T0246666

MILKWEED
and
HONEY
CAKE

MILKWEED
and
HONEY CAKE

A MEMOIR IN
RITUAL MOMENTS

WENDY A. HORWITZ

RED ⚡ LIGHTNING BOOKS

This book is a publication of

Red Lightning Books
1320 East 10th Street
Bloomington, Indiana 47405 USA

redlightningbooks.com

© 2025 by Wendy A. Horwitz

First Printing 2025

Cataloging information is available from the Library of Congress.

ISBN 978-1-68435-230-2 (hardback)
ISBN 978-1-68435-232-6 (web PDF)

In memory of my father,
whose mantra was "Be kind."

In honor of my mother,
keeper of the Friday night flame.

For my beloved children,
whose art and wit inspire.

CONTENTS

MILKWEED
and
HONEY
CAKE

Introduction

WHEN I WAS TWELVE YEARS OLD, I bailed on my bat mitzvah. Although I didn't reject Judaism per se, I thought I was an atheist, and it seemed hypocritical to perform a ritual where I'd have to intone words I didn't believe just so I could become an "adult" member of the Jewish community. Even as a younger child in Sunday school, I'd never bought into the God idea, especially since I didn't relate to the image of the guy with the white beard: too Disney, too conventional for that twelve-year-old girl who embraced women's liberation, civil rights, and the antiwar movement. So, if the Rabbi said we were praying "to G-d," I would have no part of it. The empirical world was the real thing, and the amorphous, mystical, magical, and sometimes cruel One seemed incompatible with it.

It's not that magic was absent from my childhood. I read C. S. Lewis and, half believing I would find a lamppost glowing in an icy kingdom, I squeezed between heavy winter coats and my mother's silky furs from the forties, bumped into the dark back wall of the cloak closet, and smelled—not the pines of Narnia—but moth balls and old wool. I tromped through woods behind my house and listened for sparrows and sprites. I wished on birthday candles and falling stars and even whispered to myself one blue-skied day that if God were there, he should prove it with signs and wonders. My suburban street remained quiet.

When I became an adult, part of me was sorry that no one had convinced me to have the bat mitzvah. My mother had gently suggested it might mean something to me later in life. But it was 1970; I was a child; and it appeared to me that the only option was to embrace a vintage late-nineteenth-century deity and miss out on shedding bras and the military-industrial complex.

My parents mostly let us make our own choices in matters of the heart and spirit. My father described himself as an agnostic, a word I learned early, but one that didn't seem radical enough. My mother never said explicitly, but she seemed uncomfortable talking about God. Nevertheless, they were proud of their Jewish identity, and we observed the major holidays. In fact, every Friday evening, my mother made a Shabbat dinner, and as far back as I can remember, we said the blessings over wine, challah, and candles. As teens, we were never required to be there, but into young adulthood, I found it comforting to know it was there every week. I continued the tradition with my own children.

So why did my folks observe Jewish rituals if they were agnostic or perhaps atheist? The words *tradition, identity, heritage, family,* and *community* were part of the conversation. I accepted their rhetoric and enjoyed our raucous Passover meals; my mother's Rosh Hashanah brisket; and the pomp of the temple service with the psalms and the tinkling and gleam of silver Torah finials as the leaders marched around the sanctuary, singing. The men donned their prayer shawls in near unison, with a whoosh and wave of white silk, like the setting of mainsails in a flotilla. Services were beautiful despite my boredom at the droning on, the length of it all. I even muttered some of the Hebrew prayers and sang the psalms out of respect for the people around me and because I liked different languages and old melodies in minor keys.

Even though my family enjoyed ritual without much theology, looking back, I note that no one actually suggested to me that liturgy could be something other than beseeching a personified God or that rites of passage could be other than buying into authority. Largely missing from the conversation was the possibility of engaging in ritual not necessarily in service of religious belief, but also to create beauty, solace, celebration, and community. One could find meaning through ritual without giving up one's identity or ideals. In fact, I learned much later that religious participation could enhance my own sense of identity and strengthen my convictions.

This endeavor—to discern and create meaning through ritual—is the subject of this book, a collection of essays that explore ritual through the lens of my memories and observations. The essays take a deliberately personal, subjective, and idiosyncratic viewpoint. Despite the personal perspective, I hope my reflections suggest possibilities for diverse readers to engage in meaningful rituals of their own.

Ritual is a funny thing. Actually funny. Here I am, in the twenty-first century, still shaking a bunch of branches in six directions on Sukkot (the Feast of Booths), mumbling to myself over a chunk of bread on Friday nights, wearing a tiny cap that slips off my head. Meaning does not preclude humor. Even as I engage in ritual, I hope I don't take myself too seriously. Being overly scrupulous defeats part of the purpose: to maintain our humanity. But sometimes, I am doing a ritual and feel impatient. When I've had a particularly tough week, I may not feel like lighting the Sabbath candles. I'm annoyed but try to focus on the beauty of the flowers, the silence of the house. And when that doesn't work, I look at how absurd my resentment is—against what? My own commitment to ritual? I try to remind myself that it's called a practice for a reason. Do it even when you don't feel like it, and it'll be there when you do feel like it or need it and, occasionally, you will glimpse something in the distance. This self-cajoling works. Sometimes.

Not only is ritual hard to sustain, but it also doesn't always do its job and sometimes fails us altogether. A ritual may seem to provide solace or closure, but hours or days later, a sense of something unresolved creeps in. A hard breakup? A death? Confusion about a relationship or despair about the state of the world? The emotions come around again, often at an anniversary, so one may need to repeat a ritual or a version of it over time. Perhaps this is the wisdom of formal practices that we're supposed to repeat daily, weekly, monthly, or yearly: we have an opportunity to refresh ourselves in the face of persistent trouble. Moreover, rituals for happy occasions bear repeating to remind us to live well and fully, to enjoy life.

In this book, I define ritual as ranging from established customs, such as those associated with mourning to practices that we discover outside received custom and acts we choose to frame as ritual. Indeed, some of the essays may initially seem unrelated to ritual, but I suggest that we may ritualize even seemingly mundane acts or milestones and imbue the event with delight, poignancy, and meaning. There are, though, boundaries to my definition. Not everything is a ritual. For example, daily exercise may be a salutary routine, but I would not call it a ritual.

Most humans need something beyond the empirical, partly because a sense of meaning conferred through ritual sustains us through loss, tragedy, strife, and loneliness. When I was teaching, my medical and undergraduate students spontaneously wrote about and discussed liminal moments in their lives and how they tried to frame the unbearable and mark the felicitous. They responded with enthusiasm when we acknowledged the importance of ritual and meaning. When difficulties come, those without a frame for meaning may feel particularly lost. Practical help and emotional support, though necessary, don't fully get us through. For example, a ritualized funeral not only comforts but also marks us humans as more than water and bone.

Ritual also imbues celebrations with something more lasting than champagne and cake. A big party may feel empty without ritual to highlight the transient, happy, and sad nature of life. Further, rituals for seemingly small transitions and everyday acts can lend meaning to life and make it more than a grind.

As a clinical psychologist, I understand the psychiatric benefits of communal and solo rituals and the importance of meaning in sustaining mental health. But here, I choose not to reduce ritual to a psychological phenomenon or mental health practice, though I do allude to those possibilities. Social science research on these experiences, like the data on humor or love, offers insights but fails to capture the phenomenological moment, the feeling of it. The magic.

Not magic in the sense that if I engage in ritual, the world will physically change but, rather, that we may experience a moment of transformation. Whether in major life events or in modest acts, formal and informal rituals hint at a richness akin to the child's world, hidden in the back of a coat closet, a glimmer in the woods, something potentially transcendent and imminent, whether informed by a notion of God or not.

Some of the rituals I describe in the book arose from my own acute necessity, some from serendipity, and with some, I realized only in hindsight that a ritual had taken place. Just as I adapted traditions to my needs or realized that something I was doing had the potential for ritual, so, I hope readers will find inspiration or a spark of recognition to manage difficult times or celebrate the best. Readers may already have an array of rituals or choose to create new ones, but they should feel free to borrow and adapt mine, too.

Several of the essays refer to Jewish ideas. Over time, I have turned more often to my own tradition, interpreting events and practices in that framework or discovering that some of my practices had Jewish parallels or origins. This emphasis adds layers of meaning for me. Perhaps practices that have a history make it easier to create a sense of meaning, but perhaps those we create de novo or adapt from existing ritual do this as well. Some chapters explore the possibility of creating new rituals.

Regardless of readers' religious inclinations, I trust they will recognize a deeper resonance beyond the particularities of my heritage. Rituals need not have religious content to add an exciting dimension to life, and I include both secular and religious experiences. But even that distinction has a welcome ambiguity, as I hope readers will appreciate.

1

Polishing the Silver

I'M PROBABLY ONE OF THE FEW people who actually likes to polish silver. It's tedious and should be done every time you use the silver. You end up with stinky, tarnish-stained fingers and a sore wrist. But it's also a pleasure.

When we cleared out my mother's house in 2018, I kept some of my grandmother's silver pieces with their monogrammed G for her married name, and a few of my mother's. The silver was mostly tarnished, so after returning home, I polished it: back and forth on both sides of a slender fork, counterclockwise around the curve of a candlestick base, in a spiral inside a fruit bowl. As I polished, dents and nicks in my grandmother's flatware emerged, palimpsests of a century of use. Some looked like bite marks. There was something both primal and touching about this physical evidence of long-gone relatives, the silver so delicate it yielded to a great-great aunt's dainty nibble. Or maybe a firebrand uncle waved his fork, emphasized a point, and then chomped exuberantly on a piece of beef brisket—and the fork.

Before holidays and other special meals at my house, I slide the silver from its royal-blue protective robes, scrub it vigorously with a gray anti-tarnish cloth, and buff it with a blue finishing one. The pieces take on a molten gleam, and I fall into a dreamy state. Later, when I walk by the set table, reflections of flowers, china, and the view out the window shimmer in the mirrors of silver.

I treat my china, crystal, and linen with similar ceremonial precision and enjoy setting the table with care: at Thanksgiving, a centerpiece of apples, pears, and grapes heaped in a gleaming glass bowl and dotted with fresh chrysanthemums; at the Jewish New Year (Rosh Hashanah), honey in china ramekins decorated with apple motifs; at Passover, a bottle of red wine in a lattice silver wine coaster.

Why go to the trouble, though, of polishing the silver, wiping barely discernible spots from crystal wine stems, using linen that requires special cleaning, and eating from plates that require handwashing?

A television special about Queen Elizabeth years ago showed table dressers preparing for a state dinner. They drew small measuring sticks from their waistcoats to ensure the silver, china, and napkins were perfectly symmetrical along the lengthy table. I feel like those table dressers when I tilt my head this way and that to make sure the candles are straight. I enjoy lining up the silver and napkins the same distance from the edge of the table, though I eyeball rather than measure, and I find pleasure in folding and placing linen napkins so that the embossed pattern is the same around the table. I have neither a ruler nor a waistcoat, and my guests aren't heads of state, but as I create a festive experience, I honor my ancestors and guests. Besides, preparing the table resonates with old rituals.

As with established rituals, these objects require special handling; the process may be time-consuming and serves little practical purpose; and perhaps most important, beauty deepens the meaning of the act. Theologians note that aesthetics of practice may enhance or give rise to religious experience. While beauty isn't *necessary* to ritual, we humans like beautiful things, and gorgeous objects may help us touch the sacred now and then.

In Judaism, making a ritual more beautiful than needed is called *hiddur mitzvah*—literally beautifying the deed—for example, decorating a challah cover or Kiddush cup. Scribes who create hand-lettered Torah scrolls often ornament each letter and may even decorate their handmade quill pens, rendering the calligraphic act itself meaningful. A quintessential account of hiddur mitzvah appears in Exodus (35:1–38:20), which describes the building of the *mishkan* (tabernacle). The verses themselves are beautiful, lush with descriptions of lapis lazuli, acacia wood, and blue and crimson wool.

Many traditions hold beauty to be intrinsic to the sacred. In the early 2000s, I visited Istanbul and was deeply moved by the interiors of mosques. Not only the famous Sultan Ahmed Mosque but also tiny neighborhood mosques contained exquisite tile work, prayer rugs, lamps, and calligraphy. Contemplating the tessellated tiles was revelatory.

When we make our table and its preparation more beautiful than necessary, it may reflect particular traditions, as well as basic human values. Laying out the china and polishing the silver expresses some of what is good in the world, maybe providing a spark of defiance against inhumanity and cruelty. Gilding mundane acts with intention and beauty may not rectify the world's problems, but it does help us make sense of life and imbue it with meaning.

Not only beauty but also the infrequency with which we use these pieces adds to the meaning. We create a distinction, demarcating ordinary from celebratory or sacred time, mundane preparations from potentially ritualistic acts. We make boundaries around a special time and acknowledge time itself with different table settings.

The pandemic brought this into sharp relief. During the days of isolation, time seemed to blur and shift, and we had no one with whom to share a beautiful table. So, when my family finally could gather for Passover, I went to extra trouble, creating a boundary between this time and that, in part, by laying out a satiny, hundred-year-old, peach-colored linen banquet cloth. Ritual foods and wine would stain the cloth, and it was a pain to clean, but using this old gift from a late, dear family friend, whose mother had given it to her, was worth it. In the darkening afternoon, I lit candles in gleaming silver holders and placed them on the tablecloth, marking not only the difference of the day as a holiday but also illuminating the exquisite gifts of being together and of our very lives.

In describing my table preparations, I mention peaceful, meditative states, joy, and meaning; some of my friends, however, find the mere thought of holiday preparations a trial that induces panic or perhaps narcolepsy. I get it. If I contemplate the spring holidays during January, I, too, feel like taking a nap. Some say just gathering everyone together is what matters (or they just prefer to avoid family at holidays), and many do not have the luxury of time and money to treat these preparations as pleasurable acts yielding profundities. Social comparisons can also make us feel we need to have clever napkin folds and hand-stamped name cards or something like that.

I am not suggesting that those who find all this to be a chore or those who choose simple celebrations don't create meaning, or that all rituals must be fancy. Indeed, the Society of Friends avoids ornamentation in houses of worship as contrary to the Quaker principle of simplicity, although the crisp lines; bare, softly colored walls; and aged wooden benches in meeting houses, for me, have a transcendent quality. But, even a modest act, say, shining and using one sugar spoon from a favorite aunt, might enhance the experience. Buying, seasoning, basting, fretting over, and carving a turkey is work, but using my poultry shears with their embossed handles adds another dimension.

I try to imagine my ancestors preparing festive tables. Given how much more work it was, those women might have found my interpretations overly romantic. We twenty-first-century people can open store-bought chicken stock or pop stainless flatware into the dishwasher. Do we promulgate a myth when polishing the silver?

When my children were small, I read them a beloved book from my childhood, *All of a Kind Family*, which depicts an idealized Jewish American family in the early part of the twentieth century. While charming, the book struck me in adulthood as showing a saintly mother who never complains about all the work of preparing for holidays while caring for five daughters in starched white pinafores; meanwhile, Papa goes off to synagogue. Of course, she has no dishwasher or canned chicken broth.

So, I do not want to idealize nor presume to know my matriarchs' state of mind; indeed, some could barely afford a chicken. Nevertheless, I imagine that some found moments of private joy in the objects and preparations. And whatever our differences across time, I identify with those women, for I do most of the preparations alone.

My glassware aren't heirlooms but still require care. They rest on the top shelves of a corner cabinet in my dining room. I climb carefully onto a chair to slowly draw out two stems at a time. Sometimes the wine glasses ping against each other, sending a bell tone into the depths of the cabinet, a tall and heavy piece with glass mullions that create an illusion of lightness. The front is bow-shaped to accommodate extra storage, and small hidden drawers cradle my children's animal-shaped birthday candle holders and other shiny trinkets. The cabinet was created by a Bucks County woodworker in the 1990s, and the inside smells pleasantly of aging eastern walnut wood.

I think every china cabinet has a distinct scent: my mother's heavy, carved one that used to sit in the corner of her dining room, a friend's corner cabinet filled with pottery from Japan, a sideboard found at a yard sale. A master perfumer could describe the blend of cleaners and polishes used over time or a cedar block in a linen drawer or, perhaps, the faint scent memory of a house and its inhabitants.

In addition to the corner cabinet, an antique breakfront sits in my dining room. It holds a small painted wooden box filled with cracked cinnamon sticks, a vanilla bean, cloves, and a specific bittersweet memory of mine. Inside the little box, the scent is as strong as it was a quarter century ago, and you can smell it faintly when you open the breakfront. The cabinet as a whole also smells of something I can't identify, an aroma that came with the piece. Odors have surely been absorbed into the wood of our cabinets, but maybe something else has too.

Physicists and musicians tell us that the tone of stringed instruments improves by being played expertly over time. Apparently, musical reverberations alter the actual molecular structure of the wood, aligning the cells into resonant frequencies that have been repeated. Maybe, just as an old cello retains a microscopic memory of Mozart, china cabinets absorb not only the smoke from extinguished birthday candles and the perfumes of the matriarchs but also the psalms and blessings sung at holidays; the angry slam of a kitchen door at the end of an evening gone sour; and the click of drawers opened and closed, opened and closed by the tiny, honey-smeared hand of a child looking for magic.

In a sense, the original trees still live in my dining room cabinets, in the figures of the wood, in their heft and smell, in the way they've settled into the uneven wood floor and list slightly to the tune of the old house, almost as if they've put down roots. Just as trees retain in their inner rings and cambium evidence of rain, drought, and fire, so, perhaps, our cabinets retain our histories, too—the felicitous and the sorrowful—along with the smell of beeswax candles and furniture polish.

My cabinets mirror trees in other ways. A crystal pitcher refracts the light in the dappled depths, sending out butterflies of prismed color. The shelves branch, holding the weight of my parents' grasshopper-motif ceramics from Japan. Over the years, behind the latticed wood doors, the birds, leaves, and flowers on three old, hand-painted plates have settled on branches of decades-long memories.

My small collection of "good" china rests most of the year on the bottom shelves of the corner cabinet; each size of dish has a separate home in padded cases. I unzip the cases, anticipating the riot of colors and motifs I get to see a few times a year. I don't have matching china. It's a mélange of styles I've collected over time, each pattern evoking a place, a time, a person. The gathering of place settings is barely enough for eight people.

One dinner plate is white with barely discernable gold edging and a faded green bamboo detail. It's part of a single, incomplete set, the last one from a full collection my parents had bought in Japan in the early fifties at the end of my father's deployment during the Korean War. In later years, rather than handwashing after every Passover and Thanksgiving dinner, my mother popped the china into the dishwasher, which scoured away the pattern. These were their good dishes until they were replaced by a set of plain white mid-century minimalist ones. Seeing this pattern tugs at visceral memories—eating my grandmother's matzah ball soup and my mother's plum cake, laughing and playing in a living room that resides at the edges of my memories from the house I lived in before the age of five.

Another solitary setting is diminutive, with a gold-and-dark-blue rim, which my late mother-in-law gave me one year at Christmas. It was her mother's. The teacup is translucent with a tiny handle and holds less than half of a twenty-first-century cup of coffee. I imagine Liz's Victorian father in his high, starched collar accepting a cup of tea that her mother poured out. When I see this setting in a spot of honor at one end of the table, I think of Liz, who valued legacy and knew this would be more valuable to me than any shiny, new, impersonal object. Perhaps she also knew that the china set might prompt family stories. In setting that place, I imbue our gathering with meaning and memory.

"Are you registered? Have you chosen your pattern?" Does anyone ask that question anymore? In some modern views, deliberating over place settings and coffee makers denotes wasteful consumerism or carries an acrid scent of "bride price," but whether it's popular or not, to "choose a pattern" is an intriguing phrase. You select place settings you intend to live with, along with your spouse, for the rest of your life. For some contemporary couples, choosing and receiving a pattern has been extracted from customs of dowry and price to create a meaningful ritual, the stacks of matching plates promising years of vibrant celebrations.

Despite two divorces, I still believe in such commitments and expect couples will continue setting the table with the same pattern over the years, perhaps chipped or faded along the way but still serviceable, until death do they part.

But it's quite a commitment. The china, I mean.

When a contemporary of mine turned sixteen, her mother apparently had her choose a pattern and then bought her a piece or two every year. I was surprised that she made the decision so young because one's taste often changes over a lifetime; moreover, I wondered what a future spouse might think. The choice seemed a burden to put on a teenager, but perhaps that was part of the implicit point: the ritual of choosing a pattern not only marks maturity but is also maybe intended to spur it.

What nagged me, though, was the assumption that the girl would get married at all. Indeed, why should marrying people get all the prizes? Why not choose and receive a pattern for your thirtieth birthday or school commencement? A friend told me recently that when she got divorced and bought a house, she had a housewarming and registered for new dishes. I like the idea of marking adult phases of life, whether or not one is betrothed.

And what became of the sixteen-year-old? When I heard the story thirty years later, she seemed happy about her early decision. She got married, and I believe she still used her rose-motif floral set. Same pattern, same husband.

But one must discern a lot in this process—cream versus white, gold-rimmed or not, abstract or representational, traditional or modern—and choosing a pattern may be more than a matter of taste or ergonomics, a symbol of engagement, or a reinforcement of it. As with china, people set patterns as couples or individuals. Psychologists from an earlier era told us we choose and set our patterns very early in life, although modern views permit us the grace of change and agency.

So, maybe choosing a china pattern echoes a more profound kind of pattern in life. If so, where does that leave me, with my mismatched dishes? As actual objects, rather than overladen metaphors, my plates are conversation starters. One guest has my mother's bamboo and gold, the other, a burgundy-rimmed Wedgewood; another, a fifty-year-old plate adorned with birds and flowers from the Armenian quarter in Jerusalem. All hold stories. People are charmed by the lively array of patterns on the table. And I not only wanted all those different patterns but also actively rejected the idea of selecting only one. If you squint, maybe it was partly a feminist assertion, not wanting to conform to what was expected, but it was mostly a robust belief that we should be able to enjoy many different styles, even at once if we want to.

On the other hand, is committing to a pattern such a bad thing? What if I had committed early and stuck with one pattern? One career? One partner? Maybe I would have saved myself some angst. But I now believe that I would've done as I eventually did: changed things along the way out of desire and necessity. Perhaps my hodgepodge of china patterns reflects my inclination to leave possibilities open and make changes that feel right to me.

In fact, there is a pattern in my life, but one seen only in retrospect. My pattern is one of variety and change, but like the steady tick and whir of a grandmother clock in the background, certain commitments and passions recur. My pattern is perhaps less akin to a Tiffany place setting and more like the repetition and figure-ground of a patchwork quilt. When you step back, the plates on my table reveal theme amid variation.

If my holiday preparations and the objects on my table glimmer with meaning, a few hold very particular legacies. One silver serving plate with a delicate scroll around the rim is engraved, "Mrs. Belle Weisen/President, Gotterer Family Circle/1945." My mother used this plate for cookies and cake when I was a child, but I'd never thought about the inscription much until I took it out recently. Belle was my maternal grandmother. The Family Circle was one of many organizations popular among immigrants in the late nineteenth and first half of the twentieth century. What began as burial societies to save for interment became social clubs as well, with large family gatherings.

This commemorative plate is more than a period piece; it's a testament to her volunteer spirit. Nestled in that same blue-felt silver keeper is a small fruit bowl. It is inscribed with my father's name and "Junior Chamber of Commerce/Distinguished Service Award/1961." Like my grandmother in New York, my father, in our small New England town, had pitched in. I have no idea what service merited this award, but my father and a musician friend started the town's civic orchestra, and after my father's death, I learned that he served pro bono on the municipal boards of public health and other agencies. And somewhere, there's a yellowed newspaper clipping with a photo of my mother and a brief story about her presidency of the Women's Auxiliary at the local hospital, although I've found no commemorative pieces.

The silver bowl and plate are pitted, bent, and tarnished beyond polishing, and they will likely end up in a junk shop or yard sale or eventually sold and melted down for reuse. Wherever they end up, these objects will likely be lost to the family, and the stories and charitable acts of my ancestors obscured through time.

But for now, caring for and using them evokes a legacy and honors my forebears' memory.

At a recent Thanksgiving, I mentioned family silver to my thirty-something nephew and his wife. They smiled politely. Perhaps there's little interest in all that polishing. Nevertheless, I imagine someone in the next generation or so shining one piece of silver or folding one peach-colored linen napkin, and when they hold the object at least briefly, maybe they'll tell stories or wonder about them. Caring for this bowl, this plate, infuses the stories with power. And then, after the stories have been told once more, the silver can slip away, glimmering with promise for a stranger.

2

Yellow School Bus Moments

WHEN MY SON TURNED SIX, he rode the yellow school bus for the first time. We stood at the corner with other families. He was biting his lip, with an expression of bravado mixed with worry. A new, bright-red backpack, big enough to grow into, drooped below the back pockets of his pants, and when another child spoke to him, he looked shyly at his brand-new Blue's Clues sneakers. I surreptitiously took slow, deep breaths and tried to quell the rush of adrenaline, the pounding of my heart.

The bus made a wide arc around the corner, groaned to a halt, and the door opened with a squeal. After a lingering hug, my son clambered up the steep steps.

I could see his little face pressed against the window, and I waved madly. The bus turned the corner, the light changed, and it was silent, the traffic stilled for a moment. I dabbed at my eyes, and my neighbor, who had four children, said, "I know," and put her arm around me. "It gets easier."

But "easier" isn't exactly what happened over time and circumstances. That morning, my feelings were more complicated than just anxiety or sadness, more than something to get used to.

The day my son started daycare had been different, probably closer to what my neighbor assumed I was feeling. I'd dropped

Noah off with the requisite supply of diapers, wipes, change of clothes, and lunch box. In the classroom, he was tearful and clung to me, but the caregiver gave me a hug, gestured that I should leave, took my eleven-month-old son's hand, and brought him to sit with her on a colorful rug. I stood outside the classroom, out of sight, listening to her talk softly and engage him in play, but when I left the building, I needed a caregiver. The sight of the playground made me sob, and I wandered around the neighborhood, not sure what to do next.

I was purely and simply missing my warm little one as soon as I handed him over, but that visceral sense of separation—the fear, longing, missing, worrying—was eventually soothed by time and, especially, by seeing the delight my child soon showed in making friends, bringing home gluey glittery craft projects, learning to climb and fall. Yes, it got easier. He and I were experiencing the primal, healthy attachment and separation that psychologists talk about.

The school bus was different, for while I felt a similar, sharp tug at my heart when he boarded the bus, I also simultaneously and unexpectedly experienced something else in equal measure. The bus stop was the first time I consciously felt this novel mix, though I suspect it had happened in small ways during the previous six years. At the bus stop, my mix of feelings included the familiar yearning and some sadness, but added to this was an exquisite joy and pride in my child's little departure. That doesn't quite capture the feeling; it is joy and pride tinged with a tug of separation, but more than that.

With each turn of the season, that feeling deepened and became more complex, and I came to think of these as the yellow school bus moments.

My younger child, Chrys (who uses they/them pronouns), was probably nine years old when I first saw them fall from thirty-five feet in the air. Well, not "fall" exactly: technically, it's called a "drop" in circus argot. Their limbs were wrapped in various

ways in a piece of silk fabric at a circus class, and they didn't fall
on the ground. But still. They *fell* out of the air, bounced on the
end of the silk, and hung suspended like Charlotte in her web.

Chrys had tried dance class, basketball, soccer, but when they
first walked into our local circus school, their eyes lit up. "I want
to do that, Mommy," they said in awe. Soon, Chrys was balancing
barefoot on a large rubber ball, flipping their tiny body around
a trapeze, and yes, doing a "drop." First, they climbed high in
the air and wrapped the fabric around their torso and legs, an
intricate process like macrame for a giant. And then, they let the
silk loose. With their body in balletic form, they made their way
staccato, then legato, down the fabric as if part of a child's Jacob's
ladder toy. Chrys and their classmates had tried all the circus
arts: balance, acrobatics, clowning, dance, and aerials. But once
Chrys had a choice, they wanted to be up in the air, weaving intricate wraps, climbing efficiently and gracefully like an inchworm,
as if hoisting one's own weight was no big deal. And trying and
trying again, until the palms of their hands were blistered from
rope and trapeze and fabric, and a few minor bruises showed up.
But to them, that was no big deal.

At one of the first scheduled circus exhibitions (similar to re-
citals in dance class), I sat with the other buzzing parents. Chrys
was to do an aerial solo. An actual hush fell on the crowd when
the spotlight illuminated my young child, with their elegant posture and chin held high, standing next to a forty-foot-high rope.
The music began. Chrys smoothly executed a sinuous climb to
the top, did several tricks in quick succession, and then, limbs
extended, body wrapped in silk, suddenly—it was a triple-star
drop—my child seemed to roll down the fabric. People gasped
and clapped. A mother next to me whispered, "Aren't you petrified when they do that?"

But I wasn't petrified. Thrilled, amazed, but not scared. It was
a yellow school bus moment, a sense that this child was doing
something merely yards away from me but in a place where I

could never accompany them. (And they certainly didn't get it from me. I get dizzy on merry-go-rounds.) This was their path, their passion and, while I'm sure my mouth was open and the distance from ground to ceiling seemed enormous, that moment also gave me gratitude and joy that they could literally fly on their own.

Perhaps the complex feelings in the yellow school bus moments come from this. Just as we start to get to know these little creatures—for they seem to have barely arrived—they start to leave, as it should be. But here's the thing, and this is what distinguishes these moments from dropping the kid at daycare for the first time: accompanying the pang of separation, which fades, is a soaring joy at their wobbly but determined march up the steps of the bus. Look at them, look at them, shrugging off their chrysalises and taking wing. Look at them, with their backpacks, scurrying down the sidewalk like hatchling sea turtles from nest to crashing wave.

The exquisiteness of this sense derives from the knowledge that we have the privilege of letting go a bit more each time. My soul expands as my child lugs his too-big red backpack and climbs the steep steps of the bus, or, seventeen years later, as he heads into the interior of Iceland with a much larger backpack and two friends.

I had no idea this feeling existed quite in this way, that this is a transporting, close-to-spiritual feeling. If one is lucky. It is not merely worry nor loss or sadness at the anticipation of missing the child, but—and this is the key—this moment, and all the others that follow, are simultaneously accompanied by a counterweight of joy and amazement. So, we balance on that fulcrum of separation and celebration, peering at the children's horizons, toward which they gallop.

As parents, we know our children are often three steps ahead of us: whether it's the sudden realization that the reason the plastic stacking rings and busy boxes lie neglected on the floor is that the baby has developed way beyond those simple toys, or during their early adolescence, realizing, yes, my child is quite capable of taking the train downtown alone, and their lucid argument for doing so is part of the evidence. These are the day-to-day decisions in the rush of shoddily packed lunchboxes and lost Lego pieces—we parents are always having to stretch beyond that "comfort zone," and it's neither terrifying nor gratifying, but just the day-to-day little decisions that make up being a parent and a child. Not all are yellow school bus moments, but when they happen, we see a glimpse of something transcendent in our peripheral vision.

During his childhood and teen years, Noah sang in a choir, a subset of which toured internationally once a year. Invitations to tour depended on singing ability, not age. So, when he was twelve and had a hint of swagger in his step, he headed to South Africa with the choir. I admit suffering a nightmare or two and one three-in-the-morning panic a few weeks prior to his departure. The more seasoned choir parents informed me that my behavior was typical. But by the time he boarded the large coach to the airport, it had become a yellow school bus moment.

I have a picture of us at probably five in the morning. He's wearing the requisite choir logo windbreaker, hand resting on his large, wheeled suitcase, stuffed with formal attire and a dozen pairs of black socks (only a small, odd number of which, mixed with his friends', would make it back). He's got a confident smile; he's eager to get on the bus with his friends; and, at the time, I recall, he hugged me in a way that seemed meant to reassure me rather than him. In the photo, I've got my arm around his shoulder, but barely: you can see that I have to kind of reach to enfold him. That year, he'd grown a few inches taller than me. And the next year, it was India; then north of the Arctic Circle in Norway; and, the following year, Chile. In India, unbeknownst to me, at least before he returned, he was horribly ill for a time. I only heard post hoc his humorous take on competing for the bathroom with two fellow choristers who were equally ill. Though I was sorry he'd been sick, his tale made me again see the yellow school bus turn the corner and recede. When I look at the photo of his South Africa departure, I feel a hint of that profound mix of feelings.

Some might describe this as simply pride or joy. But if it is, it's honed or maybe enriched by a sense of bittersweet but welcome loss or separation, the sense that this is what is meant to happen, what we raised them for, and there is sanctity in that.

Sometimes, such moments are firmly rooted on the ground, involving neither forty-foot circus drops nor international airplane flights, yet the feelings are no less soaring, no less complex, and they are unanticipated. It can even happen in a seemingly routine moment in one's home. Once, Noah's teenage friends had come over to hang out. I was perhaps in the kitchen or at my desk; they were upstairs, laughing, joking, on their screens, playing music or a board game. At one point, I did what I often did: ask if I could get them a snack. Politely, but with a bit of a tolerant smile and with a tone and look that instantaneously dropped a social scrim between me and the young group, my son declined on behalf of his friends. "We'll get something later. Thanks, Mom." He waited for me to leave, and I suddenly saw the scene differently: there was the hint of the man in the boy's ironic smile, no longer embarrassed at Mom being on the scene, but nevertheless pulling away, pushing even. And unexpectedly, despite the mundane setting, it was one of those moments. I felt the distance he had placed, but I was not hurt, not excluded, not any of that. Rather, it caused a surge of joy at seeing him take his own path, seeing his individual self that was entering the world more and more, even if it was just in the exclusiveness and privacy of friendships. He signaled a growing, blessed distance, and I was no longer needed. Instead, he needed this world of his own.

I was profoundly moved to witness that. In that moment, I let go again and felt happy at his capacity for friendship and autonomy, even as I felt a twinge of loss and separation from my former place in that world.

But it was just a snack, right? Maybe.

It returned again periodically. Several years later, we sat at a table in a restaurant in Noah's college town, with his friends. He argued with me in favor of Bernie Sanders for president against my "safer" choice of Joe Biden that year. In that conversation, I witnessed him and his friends oppose me with spirit and intelligence, and I experienced that passing glint of joy and the poignant sense of the wheels turning yet again. Similarly, witnessing my children's b'nei mitzvah, I surprised myself both times by *not* crying with joy. Instead, I was mesmerized by their command of the liturgy, their poise, their awe-inspiring look-ma-no-hands, and I got that sense again. It was about them, not me. That is not surprising, but what does surprise is the intensity of feeling and the fact that such transcendent opportunities occur in small events as well large.

Each time, these emotions are somewhat unexpected, this combination of separation and departure and pulling away, melded with awe and amazement and joy. And over time, this sense is intensified and made more complex. It doesn't fade with repetition. Thank God, we don't get used to it.

These yellow school bus moments are rituals, no less than graduations and other formal events. What makes yellow school bus moments ritual? That step—onto the bus, into thin air, toward the circle of friends—maybe those feel like rituals for the children, or probably not; that is their story to tell. But it is a ritual for me because I am a witness, not the "doer." That is maybe the point: that is what makes it a school bus moment—and my experience of their step, their flight, along with the flash of recognition in that moment renders it a sacred experience, one that I eventually framed as an unplanned ritual.

I am not describing ambivalence, but astonishment, as if the click of time pauses for a second and an awareness of something

important and beautiful is shot through with yearning. The paradox is that the very feeling of impending "loss" fills me with happiness and awe. My "participation" in this ritual is the sacred act
of letting go and of witnessing a concrete expression of increasing autonomy. It is a moment of imminence. As the child steps
into the unknown, we implicitly bless the act. There should be a
prayer for that.

3

It Won't Be This Simple Next Time

AS SOON AS THE CHILDREN could grasp a coin and put it into a slot, we got them small, wooden banks for charitable donations (tzedakah). Noah's was blue with a Noah's Ark motif, Chrys's was adorned with a fanciful tree of life against an aquamarine sky.

We gave them a small allowance every Sunday, and they decided how to divide up the coins: into a piggy bank for savings, an envelope for spending, and the tzedakah box for charity. "Savings, spending, tzedakah" became a kind of chant, and the plunk of coins into the charity box, a small ritual. Early on, the allowance was spare change; as they got older, it grew, though it remained modest. As youngsters, they tended to put most of their money in charity. Although the proportion changed as they got older, tzedakah still got more of a percentage than financial literacy teachers would likely recommend. If grandparents gave the children a few bills for their birthday, they often stuffed those into their tzedakah boxes, too.

Our material security likely supported their generosity; they knew no deprivation, so they weren't squirreling away savings or spending. They were also young and naïve, but children tend to be generous when given the chance, regardless of economic status, especially when adults aren't exhorting them to do so.

At some point, my kids asked how we thought they should divide their allowance, so there was a brief discussion of personal finance, but that wasn't my purpose. Whatever their intuition to charity, it was their choice.

At the end of the Jewish calendar year, in the fall, they chose a cause. The autumn High Holidays are a period of reflection, so it seemed an appropriate time. The children uncorked the boxes, dumped the coins on the kitchen table, and slowly sorted and counted their collection. Occasionally, we'd find some unidentifiable, tiny toy detritus among the silver and copper and dust bunnies. We adults made the actual donation, rounding up and paying ourselves back with the children's collection.

Around the Jewish New Year, we'd also take the children and their piggy banks to a local bank branch. The tellers smiled as the children emptied their piggies to deposit the coins in their youth accounts. Occasionally, they'd use the contents of their spending envelope to buy a treat or a toy (and later, a Starbucks card), but none of those details stuck in my memory; they didn't seem to emphasize the spending part of this practice.

As the allowance grew, along with birthday and Chanukah gifts from the grandparents, the children also took on small paying jobs like yard work and babysitting. Bills soon crowded the coins and were hard to stuff into the boxes; besides, retrieving dollar bills from a piggy bank and a wooden box with tiny openings is an hour's exercise in frustration, so we switched to three labeled envelopes. I was sorry to see the pretty tzedakah boxes go, with their satisfying, ritualistic plink of coins into the slots, the weight of the box gaining a satisfying heft over the year. The charitable result was the same, but paper envelopes lacked the sensory and spiritual resonance of the boxes.

I didn't have a tzedakah box when I was a child, but we brought coins to our Sunday school every week to put in the classroom collection. Sometimes, our religious school teachers sent home glossy cardboard coin holders with tree motifs. We'd jam quarters into the slots at the end of each branch, accumulating shiny silver leaves on the tree. It was a satisfying task, although I didn't think of it as a ritual then. When the card was full, we'd bring it back to the synagogue, and they'd magically send it to plant trees in Israel, although I learned later that some of those "trees" may have been more symbolic than actual.

My children's instincts guided their choice of charitable projects. Early on, they wanted to buy food for people who didn't have any, so we'd explain food banks, or they wanted to build houses for people who didn't have them, so organizations that aided unhoused people received their pennies. When they wanted to protect manatees or monarchs, we'd help them select an environmental group.

In later seasons, my children deliberated over causes: books for the public library or justice equality? Freedom of speech or rain forest protection? Some years, they divided their charity between two organizations. But the very first time that Noah chose a cause, the year we first gave him the tzedakah box, the year he turned three, he didn't hesitate. "I want to buy a helicopter for Uncle Aaron's fire station," he said. He emptied his tzedakah box and tried to sort the coins.

My brother was indeed a firefighter, in Seattle, so a donation would be easy to arrange, though maybe not a whole helicopter. Like many preschoolers, Noah had entered that phase of wanting to grow up to be a firefighter; with an uncle in the business, he knew that real grownups worked this real job, so it made some sense he'd chosen this cause.

So, Noah dictated a letter, which I transcribed verbatim, telling the station what to purchase with his donation. He scribbled something that he said was his name, we enclosed a small check and dropped the letter in the mailbox. A few weeks later, he received a thank you note from the fire chief, along with a certificate of appreciation, two fire department decals, and most impressive, a sew-on-patch embroidered with the fire department's logo. Noah wore that patch on the sleeve of several seasons' winter jackets, as I carefully detached and sewed it on each time he grew out of a coat.

Perhaps what prompted my son's choice were the enormous, whizzing, red or neon green trucks with blaring sirens, the firefighters' impressive garb, the tall ladders: a child's romance with big machines and the derring-do he saw in his picture books. Maybe it was the faint knowledge that firefighters enter where others don't, the heart of what we tell children to stay away from. A stranger's car. Danger. Fire. Firefighting is a classic drama with lots of props. In my son's storybooks, in fairy tales and fantasies, danger was overcome, those in distress were rescued, and everyone lived happily ever after.

But that year, in the time he chose his first tzedakah project, the Jewish New Year arrived on a Monday. A Monday that fell six days after a Tuesday. Tuesday, September 11, 2001.

I had done everything I could to prevent my son from seeing images of the towers falling, of ash and bodies, of people running in terror or walking in a daze, of airplanes crashing. But his charitable choice seemed too much of a coincidence, a toddler's imagination about firefighters notwithstanding, his uncle's job aside. At this writing, I could not know his motivation at that time: he was too young to have registered in long-term memory the details of that period or his state of mind, so more than two decades later, we could not determine the truth. But even in those days before ubiquitous screens and the internet, something might have seeped into his awareness, something he intuited or saw, something to do with firefighters, something that had gone awry. Something requiring helicopters. Something broken that a small boy's tiny stack of quarters, dimes, nickels, and pennies—shaken out of a small wooden box and sorted and counted—could, in some small way, repair.

⟡

Dividing the allowance and earnings continued until the mitzvah years when it took a different form. Along with learning their Torah portion and the liturgy, mitzvah children at our synagogue were expected to complete *tikkun olam* projects during the year preceding their ceremony. Tikkun olam means "repair of the world," and projects could be volunteering or fund-raising for a cause. In addition, the children often educated themselves about their causes and explained their projects in their Torah commentary at the service.

As my children developed their projects, we suggested a larger-scale version of what they'd done with their allowance: to take a portion of monetary gifts they received and funds they earned that year and donate it to their cause, along with the money they'd raise for the project. As with the little box, the choice of how to distribute the funds would still be theirs: savings, spending, tzedakah.

This larger-scaled project seemed a good transition from the concrete act of collecting coins to more complex, abstract financial contributions and activism. Yet a ritual quality remained since the project developed while learning what they needed for the mitzvah religious service. It was framed in the meaning of the Torah portions they studied and in their individual commitments and choices. In the end, I watched as their donations echoed the pennies dropped into the little wooden boxes: a majority of the money they received as gifts went to their causes.

My son's project aimed to decrease his community's use of fossil fuels for six months. He offered suggestions for how to do so; obtained pledges from congregants, friends, and family; and raised money for climate change organizations. My own pledge was not to drive on Saturdays, which is Shabbat. As I began this practice, I noticed that I also started shopping less that day and making other changes that might affect the environment. On the Saturday mornings that my son attended synagogue in advance of his bar mitzvah, I often walked the two miles with him;

it was "quality time" together, and in some small way, maybe reduced pollution. But it was also meaningful to observe the Sabbath in some way: traditionally, one avoids working and "lighting a flame"—in modern terms, using machines and electricity. Friends and family described their pledges as equally thought-provoking.

I had not thought of Chrys's mitzvah project for a while, but recently, I went on a clean-out rampage, purging clothes, emptying plastic storage bins, donating old toys and books, and discarding a number of unidentifiable objects from the basement. As a rule, I don't get rid of anything in my children's bedrooms without asking, but they were supposed to have cleaned them when they moved from home, and I wanted to see what sartorial detritus remained. Actually, I had run out of clean T-shirts, it was six in the morning, and I was impatient to go for my daily walk without having to recycle a dirty tee of mine. Maybe there was an abandoned shirt in a dresser drawer that I could borrow.

Chrys's dresser contained only a blanket, some mementos, and three pairs of jeans, but in my son's second drawer, under orphaned socks, a choir logo windbreaker, and a bathing suit beyond use was a rumpled, faded T-shirt. Hoping it had been washed sometime in this millennium, I shook it out. The design jolted my memory. A rainbow-hued equal sign—the "marriage equality" symbol—was hand-painted on the front, and on the back, in hand-blocked letters was the word "Brother." I suddenly remembered the three of us decorating those tees, with Noah drawing the equal signs in brilliant hues, and Chrys and me painstakingly writing the block letters for "Brother," "Mom," "Dad," and "Chrys" on four different shirts.

We'd created these tees for the culminating event of Chrys's project, advocacy and fund-raising for the campaign for marriage equality. Early in the year, Chrys, then twelve years old, met with friends of ours who were lawyers, one a specialist in international human rights. The couple were also gay so they might have personal knowledge of discrimination and advocacy. They gave Chrys a mini tutorial on the history, law, and social and political issues relating to marriage inequality and gay rights, as well as possible opportunities for activism and fund-raising. I sat in another room while Chrys took careful notes and asked lots of questions. There was also warmth, tea, and laughter at the table. Chrys then wrote letters to representatives and local publications and gave a talk in the community, raising awareness and money for the Human Rights Campaign and for the American Civil Liberties Union.

But Chrys also wanted to do something tangible that would dramatize and celebrate the equal rights campaign. They began planning an event, designing and posting flyers and online notices and contacting local newspapers and other publications. A few months into planning, a local news organization called and wanted to interview this twelve-year-old whose one-person campaign had caught the imagination of a reporter. The publicity snowballed, with other organizations and websites picking up Chrys's story.

The event would be an art project in the parking lot of our synagogue. Friends, family, congregants, neighbors, and the wider community were invited to come on a Sunday to create an enormous street mural in colored chalk. We would be asked to draw what "love" meant to us. With a bit of coaching, Chrys met with administrators at the synagogue to make logistical arrangements, talked with artist friends about how to stage the project, gathered tables and other materials, and even made sure their brother would film and photograph the event to document and post it online, encouraging future donations and awareness.

Although Chrys's mitzvah would not be until September, they wanted the project to be in mid-June, when they would turn thirteen.

That Sunday morning was clear and beautiful, cooler than the typical muggy Philadelphia late spring day. We donned our T-shirts and arrived early to set up. Friends showed up with toddlers who drew enormous, wobbly hearts. We'd set up snacks, beverages, festive music, and big jars for donations. Chrys's uncle, a trained artist, drew a fanciful landscape with rainbows. Inspired by flyers, articles, and a letter Chrys had written for the synagogue newsletter, some people who had never met Chrys showed up. "That such a young person would care—I've been in my committed relationship with my partner for thirty years—this is remarkable," said one woman. Some wrote slogans or personal statements in large, colorful letters: "Marriage equality now!" "Love is love!" A child and their two moms drew a simple picture of three figures next to a tree, with a dialogue bubble above the child: "This is our loving family." Chrys flitted from group to group, to children to grandparents, to a loudspeaker we'd set up so that they could thank people and invite them to donate.

When we arrived at religious school two weeks later, students and teachers hurried to Chrys and congratulated them with high fives, whoops, and hugs. The rabbis came to cheer as well. Chrys was puzzled and somewhat embarrassed. "What did I do?" Chrys asked. Didn't you hear, everyone said. It passed! That day, June 26, 2014, the US Supreme Court struck down bans on same-gender marriage, making it legal in all fifty states.

With gentle irony, several of the adults said, hey, don't expect it to be so simple next time! But Chrys had done their research and knew that this had been decades in the making. Besides, the project didn't come out of nowhere: they'd always had an intuitive, passionate sense of indignation about unfairness and cruelty in the world, and that would continue.

Their Torah reading contained the verse, "*Tzedek, tzedek, terdof.*" "Justice, justice, pursue it." "Terdof" connotes *pursuit* in the fiercest sense of the word, and "tzedek" has the same root as "tzedakah." In that phrase, charity and justice are one.

When Chrys offered their final version of commentary at the service on a September Saturday, we heard them link activism, change, and the pursuit of justice to Torah. Acts similar to my small, local campaign, Chrys said, were small drops in an ocean, but if enough of us created such drops, we could form a wave and a sea change.

By September, rain and traffic had blurred the chalk drawings beyond recognition. The rainbow colors faded and washed away into the parking lot drains. In the years that followed, we saw the hope of that era blur and fade as well: the human rights campaign was not over, especially not in the intervening decade, when that act of justice, along with other human, civil, and constitutional rights, were battered and erased by terrible storms of violence and vitriol.

But the image of one child wanting to buy a helicopter and a young teenager trying to change a law with a chalk drawing helped sustain me through cynicism and despair.

4

The Swamp

NEAR THE HOUSE WHERE I GREW UP was an area my mother called "the bayou," what we children called "the swamp." It was a New England wetland, really. The swamp held magic: skunk cabbage that jutted its alien-looking leathery leaves and engulfed you with its rank odor when you stepped on it and fern fiddleheads that reemerged each spring and unfurled slowly until you could run your fingers under the fronds and coat your skin with gold dust. And rare and most wonderful, wild orchids, glowing pink in the shade. I'd kneel on the damp moss, soaking the knees of my blue jeans, and peer into the orchid's bulbous lip to watch for bees staggering out. Very early—so early, it seemed I'd always known it—my mother taught me this "lady slipper," *cypripedium*, took more than ten years to first bloom, and if we picked or pulled it out, it would be gone. It didn't transplant. It didn't come back. When I found one, I felt something elusive, something like awe. I recall an older boy and I hanging out in the swamp, and he deliberately stepped on or maybe yanked out an orchid. I yelled at him, in tears; it felt mean, bad, wrong. And when I later learned that those orchids became endangered, the subsequent loss of the wetlands near our house—along with the orchids—seemed a desecration.

I also spent hours wandering the deciduous woods beyond my backyard. In a clearing where the highway and the neighborhood dogs were a distant lull, I'd daydream on a thick bed of soft pine needles, absently crush and smell wild wintergreen leaves and chew on their minty red berries, watch the wavering pattern of leaves in shadow and light against the sky, listen for chipmunks and foxes rustling through the underbrush. Threaded through the oaks and maples was something that filled me with joy and yearning.

Magic. Awe. Yearning. Perhaps these are among the conditions for ritual to emerge.

I suppose most children have a hidden world in their imaginative play, maybe even a spiritual feeling. Or perhaps it's a desire to believe in a hidden world. For me, this desire rippled across ponds, flashed in the poppy epaulets of red-winged blackbirds, and most of all, lived in the determined step and gold-patterned dome of box turtles.

Every spring, I'd find at least one, and in the spacious, chicken-wire pen my father built, I'd tend them over the summer, spend hours watching them root around in the leaves, eat, bump into each other. At first skittish, they'd seal themselves into their shells when I approached, but after a few days, they'd get to know me, or so I thought, and they would slowly open their hinged plastrons, extend their ET-like necks, and stare at me, their beaked mouths turned down in a permanent "harrumph." From my hand, they'd eat caterpillars, berries, leftover lettuce leaves; they even bit into American cheese, and their pointy mouths left a scalloped edge. I scattered pine needles and twigs for them to burrow in and left a small, overturned box with an opening for shelter, which some of them took to. And in the fall, I picked them up, whispered something like a spell or a prayer, and set them down where they'd originally emerged from the woods. Then, faster than the fables claimed, they marched straight in the direction of the nearby reservoir, where I imagined they buried themselves to hibernate.

I don't know if letting them go at the end of the summer was a ritual, but the turtles and their arrival and departure filled me with awe and a sense of magic hidden in the woods. And when I learned later that there were global legends and religious beliefs about turtles, it made perfect sense. I loved the idea of a great turtle holding up the whole world.

The realm of orchids and turtles hinted at meaning and transcendence, while the religion of my childhood offered a liturgical and theological background that I took for granted but ultimately absorbed. And in my twenties, I began to appreciate alternative views of religious rituals and the possibilities for secular ritual. The intervening decades have deepened my sense of these possibilities, and even my fixed notions of "God" have gotten fuzzy around the edges. As for turtles, they remain a source of amazement.

5

Spring Cleaning

BEFORE PASSOVER, IT'S TRADITIONAL to give away bread and meticulously clean the house because the observance includes eating only unleavened starches during the week, and the home is supposed to be free of leftover breadstuffs. I didn't grow up with the full practice. Instead, the day before the holiday started, my mother piled half-loaves of bread into the freezer and stuffed crackers and cereals into a cabinet, then sealed it all with a piece of masking tape. Maybe it was a symbolic demarcation of a non-Passover zone; I'm guessing the tape was also meant to stop us kids from grabbing Cheerios and white bread by mistake. But years later, when my children were in elementary school, I decided we'd actually deep clean our kitchen if not the whole house.

First, we used up freezer-burned ends of bread, macaroni shards at the bottom of the box, and sugary remnants of Frosted Flakes cereal. The kids clambered onto the counters to wipe the tops of the fridge and the high shelves; we discarded old spices that had lost their oomph and condiments that had congealed and hidden in the backs of cupboards. The evening before Passover began, per custom, we went through the house by candlelight, using a feather to gather crumbs from window sills. The feather dusting was a kind of scavenger hunt for the children, and they raced from room to room to find tiny pieces of bread I'd planted for their benefit. The kitchen was close to pristine, and the kids reveled around our miniature bonfire of the crumbs on the porch the next morning.

That spring cleaning heralded our family's ritual meal the next evening, with its flavors of sharp horseradish, sweet chopped apples, and crunchy matzahs.

I've long been intrigued that Christian Lent often coincides with the pre-Passover time, and like Passover, Lent entails purifying and abstaining before Easter. My adult friends who observed Lent sometimes gave up sweets, alcohol, or something like social media; indeed, some rid their kitchens or houses of tempting treats. Maybe the hint of warmth in the air and the faint tinge of green on tree limbs prompt our urge to clean, to start fresh.

Over the years, even as my children and I lost interest in deep cleaning the kitchen, I continued to clear out all breadstuffs and did at least some spring cleaning. In fact, as my pre-Passover ritual dwindled, its meaning swelled. I felt as if I were sweeping up the year's stagnant hopes along with the stale bread. I wiped clean a few hard-to-reach shelves—and dusty habits. I watched unfilled promises drift away with the burnt crumbs in the morning. At least, I tried to.

With its symbolic foods and ritualized tasks, the Passover meal itself commemorates the ancient Exodus from Egypt. The Hebrew word for Egypt, Mitzrayim, means "straits" or "narrow place," like the wedge of land snug between the Nile River and the Red Sea, and the word may also connote biblical slavery. In recent times, some have interpreted *narrow place* as the suffering of groups shackled with economic, social, and political oppression in our time.

But in some years, my own difficulties made it hard to focus on the problems of my contemporaries, let alone those in a remote biblical story. But maybe there are seasons to attend more to the suffering of others, and seasons to attend to our own.

In those harder times, I imagined making room at the table for a private narrow place. Sometimes, it was a loss that weighed me down, heavy as granite. Sometimes, I wanted to untie knots of despair, begin an exodus of the heart. I yearned to enter a wide, silent desert, discover an oasis sheltered with palms, their leaves softly clacking, a well of cool water.

On the second night of Passover, Jews traditionally begin counting the omer, a ritualized statement of the forty-nine days between Passover and Shavuot (Festival of Weeks, or Pentecost). One literally says, "This is the first/second/etc. day of . . ." Like many religious practices, Shavuot has ancient agricultural and biblical roots: it originally celebrated the grain harvest, but eventually marked the receiving of Torah (the Laws) and revelation at Mount Sinai.

I had never counted the omer until one spring when I needed to get beyond a harmful attachment, and the omer presented itself as a ritual for that leave-taking. I hoped it would bring me to a new place, figuratively speaking, like the ancients' actual pilgrimage to Jerusalem with their summer grain offerings.

Seven weeks seemed a long time, and this would be a solo journey, but I made a mental commitment to the practice.

Each morning, I read the simple prayer and marked the days, acknowledging any sadness and noting one thing that gave me hope. I counted the omer at the same window every day so that I could see my backyard and the bird feeders. Some days, just stating the number and looking out the window made me smile, like the morning I noticed the apple tree had begun to bloom or the day I watched hummingbirds return. Some days, though, the count brought tears or I resented it but said it anyway, with bitterness. Some mornings, I had to get over my *why am I doing this, I don't feel like it, this is ridiculous* attitude.

But that year, I counted the days, all forty-nine of them, step by step.

6

Shared Spaces

ON A MARCH EVENING SEVERAL YEARS AGO, I found my-self talking to a pockmarked, gray rock about the size of a small grapefruit. No, I had not lost my mind, though it is hard to tell this story for reasons other than embarrassment. The rock rested on a small bed of dried sage on the fireplace mantel in my living room, near a photo of my late father. It was the second anniversary of my father's death. I addressed the limestone: "Grandfather Rock," I said, acknowledging the stone's presence, then lit the memorial candle and said the prayers in memory of my father. The round stone reflected the yahrzeit candle's soft glow. My dad, generally an empiricist, might nevertheless have understood my talking to the rock.

The stone is geologically intriguing, but it is more than that. It was given to me by a Native American tribal leader during a one-week service-education trip on a reservation, where a colleague and I served as chaperones for ten college students.

One morning during the trip, ankle deep in mud, I was picking up debris near the site of an unfinished community center that we were painting. I stacked the garbage in a little pile, but the wind kept scattering it, so I asked one of the leaders for a trash bag. We found a torn plastic grocery bag wrapped around a spiky bush, and I went back to work. Soon, something distracted me. High above in a long, perfect V was a flock of birds, their long necks and streamlined bodies, brilliant white against the blue sky. The man stood next to me and watched the birds, too. "They're swans," he said, "Listen." We listened until their cries faded and the flock turned as one and disappeared. I returned to cleaning and raking.

A while later, the man picked up a spherical, gray-white rock from a small pile. I cannot recall exactly what he said. It was neither a question nor a directive, but it was clear that I was being invited to take the rock home. He told me his grandmother used stones like this in her cooking fires and that it was limestone from the hill above us. I cupped the rock in my hand, felt its weight. Perhaps I thanked him. He nodded and reached into his canvas shoulder bag for a handful of dried sage stalks. "You can rest Grandfather Rock on the sage," he said.

I imagined security at the airport questioning me about this object that probably looked like an antique cannon ball on X-ray. At the same time, I was grateful. Previously, the notion of accepting a gift like this might have raised complicated questions and a vague discomfort. The rock was sacred to my host, but did its sanctity transfer to my hands? With the actual rock in my hand, however, the questions seemed not to be the point. In fact, the man who gave me this rock might have been amused by my questions, for during that week, our small group was invited to temporarily enter the circle of this community, who welcomed us with hospitality and humor.

Receiving the grandfather rock evoked some elusive emotions. What happened the next night, though, more profoundly shifted my sensibilities.

Ironically, the experience that next evening was the thing I'd dreaded most about this trip—not the expected fifty-mile-an-hour winds, mud, and freezing temperatures, which I'd packed appropriate clothing for; not physical work, which I enjoy; and not shepherding ten inexperienced young adults, which, for me, is a fun challenge and an opportunity to learn from and get to know my students. What I dreaded most was the event we'd been told would be the highlight of the trip. The sweat lodge.

Of course, I was not compelled to participate, but I wanted at least to be available to my students and to encourage them to be open to new experiences. I was also curious. But anxiety crowded my sense of duty and curiosity. To some extent, I was uneasy because I anticipated feeling like an intruder on someone else's tradition, or that it would be a spectacle designed for tourists. Of course, all communities are entitled to distinguish private practices from public presentations, but for reasons I don't fully understand, I am sometimes embarrassed by the latter. And would I need to help my students interpret the experience, whatever it turned out to be? How would I interpret it for myself? But much more than all of that, I simply dreaded the heat. It would be hot. Very, very hot.

To say that I have never liked saunas is putting it mildly: the dry heat makes me queasy, claustrophobic, and impatient, and I expected this to be an uncontrollable sauna-like experience, soaked with my wariness. We'd been instructed to dress modestly but lightly and not to wear bras with metal clasps (they'll burn you in the heat), so in the days before the trip, I obsessed over which long, summer skirt would be comfortable and which top modest enough but not too warm.

That morning, we gathered near a low, domed structure built of willow branches and insulating cloths and blankets. We swept away water and mud that had flooded the area, cleaned debris from the interior and the surrounding ground, made small repairs to the blanketed exterior, and gathered firewood and kindling for a bonfire that would be built outside the lodge. At one point, a leader indicated that we needed more firewood and led a small group of us on foot to an area a mile or so away where we collected more fuel. Tromping up and down hills, we passed a field where several lodges and other ceremonial structures stood,

scraps of colored fabric fluttering on a pole in the wind. We returned cradling sticks and splintered logs.

Preparations took the better part of the morning. Firewood
and kindling were stacked, and blankets were placed on the
lodge's earth floor. The bonfire was lit. It would be used to heat
rocks for inside the sweat lodge.

Late in the day, we gathered around the fire. People chatted but
soon fell silent and, after a time, a tribal member asked us guests,
"What is your spirit animal?" As we made our way around the
circle, I was nervous but also knew my answer without hesitation,
and it moved me in a way I didn't fully comprehend.

It was my turn. The man looked at me with warm curiosity.
"The turtle," I said. Some of my worries started to dissipate, although the heat of the bonfire did little to quell my anxiety about
the sweat lodge's interior climate.

One by one, we ducked our heads to enter the low dome of
the lodge through a small opening covered with a cloth flap.
Warm, but not overpowering, the dimly lit space felt close, with
every sound magnified. Rocks that had been in the bonfire were
stacked in the center and created a dry heat. We sat in a circle
with our backs to the curved walls, with the leader at the covered
opening. I sat hip to hip with a local woman about my age on one
side and one of my students on the other.

The ceremony began with simple recommendations for us
newcomers, and then the lodge filled with a deep, resonant song.
The melody repeated, louder and louder, reverberating in my
chest, and I found myself breathing with the slow, steady cadence.
Silence, and an elder asked if anyone wished to speak. More silence, and the heat penetrated my skin and scalp. Sweat began
to drip down my chest and face. A woman said that her mother's
diabetes was worse. Someone told about a child struggling in
school. Two students from our group expressed appreciation for
the hospitality that week, and one said that he felt transformed
by his visit. After each speaker came a chorus from the circle, a

deep, voiced sound that rippled across the small, warm space. The transcribed "unh" does not fully convey the tone or the emotion.

Then, silence, and the leader opened the entry flap to retrieve more heated rocks from the fire. He placed them on the center pile and poured water on top. Steam hissed with a blast of heat, raising the temperature in the lodge. Another song and chant, this time by a teenager. The older people's songs, I learned later, were mostly traditional, but the boy's song was his own creation, fresh and contemporary but without obvious reference to modern music and with a melody and rhythm that seemed timeless.

I did not understand the language of the songs but felt some sense of meaning, emotion. In my tradition, when we sing a psalm or prayer rather than speak it, there are said to be two offerings and two meanings, one from the words, and one from the music. Singing perhaps expresses something ineffable: joy, anguish, or unformed sensibilities that words alone cannot convey. Similarly, the songs in the lodge seemed to transcend language.

The young man's song ended, and an enthusiastic wave of "unh-huh" rose from our hosts in the circle, the sound seeming to accept and celebrate the chant.

Seven rounds of ceremony followed: the addition of more rocks and water, steam, increasingly intense heat; a song and chant; the simple response; silence. Then more heat. And more. In the first couple of rounds, I wondered if I could tolerate the rapidly increasing temperature, like facing an open oven. But the woman next to me, noticing my discomfort, showed me how to drape a towel over my face for a minute, and while I continued to feel the heat in my body, my eyes, nose, and mouth found some temporary relief. With my legs extended toward the hot stones, my clothes were quickly soaked with sweat, but by the third round, my discomfort started to feel beside the point.

By the seventh, hottest round, I could not have cared less about my hot, soggy T-shirt, streaming forehead, and the scorching air that entered my nostrils with each breath, nor that I could see only blurred images because I had been instructed to leave my glasses outside (it would be dangerous to wear them in the heat). I felt neither claustrophobic nor anxious. Each rising chant enveloped me, and the dense, relentless heat came to feel restorative rather than depleting, like a balm rather than something to be endured.

Inside the small dome, there was a kind of intimacy. We could hear each other's breath, sense everyone's body in the small space, and it was as if we were embraced by the heat and by each other's presence. I felt as if we were all part of this circle, if temporarily.

With each round of heat, chanting, and silence, I passed through different sensations: noticing details, a kind of a meditative state, a wordless sense of something shifting, awe, no sense of time. Perhaps as religious an experience as I have ever had. At the same time, I was not just "inside myself." In fact, I wasn't thinking much at all but, rather, felt connected and attentive to those around me: the woman who handed me the towel; my student, with whom I shared a grateful glance at one point; the nods and welcoming utterances of our hosts; and a deep sense of humanity and belonging.

I was wrong in every way that I had anticipated this ceremony. Wrong in worrying about being embarrassed, wrong about needing to explain anything to my students. Wrong about the heat. And what I hadn't anticipated at all was spiritual rejuvenation. Yes, spirituality: that word I usually avoid because it's sometimes used as a euphemism for those uncomfortable with the word "religion," or it's a catch-all for vague, supernatural-sounding experiences that people describe in ways that give me the willies. But my experience was neither supernatural nor vague; I had experienced something transcendent and real and within a community—a community that was not "mine" but that seemed to welcome us visitors fully for that short time. And it was definitely not a sauna. Not something for one's health or relaxation, even if that might be a byproduct. Instead, the

experience allowed me into a world I would never have otherwise witnessed, and it opened something in myself as well.

I was chagrined at my self-indulgent worries in anticipation of
the sweat lodge. My prior thoughts, in retrospect, made all sorts
of assumptions. And if the ceremony might have differed without
us visitors, so be it.

I've attended cultural events and services in churches, mosques,
and other religious institutions outside my own, and I have visited
synagogues that were as far from my experience as the settings
outside my tradition; I've been invited to and witnessed rites of
passage in places ranging from the Pacific Northwest to Gambia,
but I have rarely felt so much a part of "someone else's" ritual. In
the sweat lodge at that time and place, the songs and prayers, the
communal affirmations, the welcoming glances of our hosts—all
of it, at that moment, seemed to belong to no one and to everyone.
We guests could partake without taking. The circle seemed as
open to us as were the generous pots of food each night.

Why? Perhaps it was the woman next to me who shared the
towel; perhaps it was hearing people's stories about their lives, or
the chants. Perhaps it was the palpable sense of connection with
the people sitting near me. Perhaps it was my students' appreciation. Perhaps it was the heat. Perhaps it was meaningful because
it was in the context of the community for whom this ritual has
long held meaning. The community engaged in this ritual frequently, within a dense web of their longstanding relationships
with each other, and the ritual is embedded in other collective
actions, beliefs, and practices, both secular and sacred. The lodge
was freestanding, but the practice was not. Perhaps we guests
could be part of the circle for that moment because, for us, it was
temporary and because we had worked alongside our hosts that
week. Perhaps that ritual was able to hold us because in that small
space, there seemed to be no room for us-versus-them.

Previous to this experience, if I had read a similar account—
spirit animals and feeling "as one," for example—I might have

been embarrassed for the narrator and cringed at what might have seemed a hippy-dippy naïveté. But in the context of this community, who frequently entered the sweat lodge together, I had been invited, and it felt natural for me to enter, too, just as it felt natural to accept Grandfather Rock and even to join a chant when invited to do so on another day. It did not feel as if I had violated a boundary, as I'd worried. Moreover, I found myself accepting my own wordless experience in the sweat lodge, alongside my usual practical way of thinking. Perhaps the acceptance of such seeming contradictions and unanswered questions is a condition for engaging in meaningful ritual: the experience is not measurable, yet it is as real as anything in the empirical world.

Over months—years actually—I weighed telling the story. It seemed risky. Risky because how could I convey experience that is so outside words? Risky also because I did not want to misinterpret something or inadvertently encourage a kind of touristic intrusion that echoes the worst of North American history relative to Native peoples.

In Judaism, the word *hevdel* ("difference") connotes a meaningful boundary, such as the demarcation between work days and the Sabbath. But I've also thought of this concept as referring to boundaries around rituals. Perhaps if we don't protect a ritual space or practice or identity, such rituals might be diluted and lose meaning. So, most of us who are not Catholic would never consider taking communion at mass just because we were curious or felt moved to do so. For related reasons, I do not rise during Kaddish, the Jewish memorial prayer, unless I am in mourning or observing an anniversary of a close family member's death, although some do so in modern practice. Further, I think that serious, uninvited intrusions on ritual boundaries can be destructive. Yet, I realize that there are rich, enduring traditions, religions, and cultures around the globe that vary in how strict or permeable such boundaries are.

Perhaps what mattered in my sweat lodge experience was the context: we were invited into the lodge's circle, and the ritual was conducted by the people for whom it is most meaningful, within the community where this practice originated. Yet I still have no definitive answers about any of this, and one needs to keep asking how and where we belong in each other's sacred spaces.

To what extent can we gain meaning from each other's traditions and rituals? What are the boundaries and the conditions for acting with respect and maintaining meaning? So, when I have invited non-Jewish guests to attend and participate in a Passover seder or when I've been invited to offer a blessing for a new baby at a christening, it seemed to work. One must ask, though, who decides and when? What is the current context and the history? I am still figuring it out.

In the sweat lodge that night, though, and during that whole week of learning and working, my sense shifted of what might be okay between communities and cultures and my view changed of how shared ritual can impart meaning to all, without necessarily eroding a community's internal sense of integrity. I cannot speak for our hosts in the sweat lodge, but for me—although I generally prefer boundaries and distinctions to sustain meaning—that moment of communion and sanctity was shared.

When we left the lodge that night, a cool, early evening breeze dried my damp face, and I retrieved my glasses from a picnic table. People chatted and laughed over a buffet of fragrant stew, fresh bread, and vegetables. Those who had not been in the lodge joined us for dinner.

I put my glasses back on, and the world was in sharp relief: the silhouettes of tree branches, a vivid sunset, birds settling for the night. I put on my sweater and accepted a steaming bowl of food.

7

Narrow Bridge

MY FIRST THANKSGIVING IN GRAD SCHOOL, in '83, I drove north from Philadelphia to Connecticut for the first time. Navigating the Charybdis of rush hour denizens and the Scylla of Thanksgiving escapees, I was soon trying to keep pace on the life-threatening New Jersey Turnpike and the claustrophobia-inducing Garden State Parkway. And then, a few miles past the border into New York State, the sky opened, and the Hudson spread to the horizons; the brown cliffs of the Palisades loomed; and the Tappan Zee Bridge rose, silvery and intricate.

The bridge and I grew up together. Three years before I was born, Chevy Bel Airs and Ford Country Squires began speeding over its new cantilever spans. The bridge was never meant to last more than fifty years because money and materials were tight after the Korean War, but in the second decade of the twenty-first century, new Priuses and Camrys hummed over this three-mile stretch of the Hudson River.

You didn't so much cross the bridge as enter its latticed girders, a baby boomer's dream of a giant Erector Set, anchored by long upsweeps to the banks of the river. In the '60s and '70s, my family would take the bridge from my childhood home in Connecticut to visit cousins in Baltimore or the museums in DC. I'd try not to blink as I watched the steel network whiz by to catch a glimpse of the little white lighthouse on the east side of the river and a flash of the Empire State Building to the south. The car tires echoed on the spans, *kerthump-kerthump.*

Place names around the Tappan Zee were magic: the Palisades sounded like a fantastical amusement park; Bear Mountain, the home of ogres and heroines; Tarrytown, an eponymous place of porches and rocking chairs. And I could see trains chugging along the river, from The City, past the legendary Sleepy Hollow, through what I imagined was wilderness and finally, Upstate, that elysian borscht belt where my grandparents forever picnic in a sepia meadow.

Once I had my own children, we'd take the Tappan Zee on our way to holidays and vacations to avoid the George Washington Bridge's glacial pace. Besides, Tappan Zee, named for the Tappan Lenape people and the Dutch word for *sea*, was fun to say. When the children were young, we'd proclaim in some made-up accent, "Tap on zee bridge," as if we could touch it like a child's play set. Rolling onto the first span, we'd belt out Arlo Guthrie and Pete Seeger's anthem to the Hudson, "Sailin' Up, Sailin' Down," with one of us doing the call, the others, the response—up/down, down/up, fish/hell, hell/fish—and the children shouting "hell" at the crown of the bridge.

One of the pleasures of crossing was to see what was visible in the distance. If it was clear to the south, the silver-gray silhouette of the Chrysler Building, sometimes a glint of a window; if it was misty, a wash of skyline, maybe a spire poking through the clouds. You needed the perfect angle to get a full view of New York City, and even then, it was a shooting star's worth of time in my peripheral vision.

To the north of the bridge where the river bends, as I'd tell the children, we could imagine a stretch of whistle-stop towns and Hyde Park with its smiling, pearl-adorned Mrs. Roosevelt and her cigar-puffing husband. Sometimes I viewed the steep

Palisades through the lens of the Hudson River School's romantic painterly vision.

But the bridge was not without its shadows. The Wednesday of Thanksgiving week in 2001, the sign for the bridge filled me with dread. My son was a toddler, my younger child, a baby. At the crown, I glanced south and saw—nothing—just the gaping wound of sky where the Twin Towers had been.

A private ritual took hold. Without a word, I'd regard the empty space above the city each time we crossed as though in pilgrimage. Even when the new fraternal twin towers emerged from the skyline, I still nodded to the old towers' ghosts, which hovered in the clouds.

But there was grace from the sweep of the bridge. Sailboats leaned into the wind; barges plowed upriver. In severe winters, the Hudson could freeze in great chunks of ice that bumped against each another, waves lapping them along like in the Arctic.

The bridge still beckoned through the summer of 2017, but it would soon be gone, replaced by a sturdy leviathan with a planned hundred-year lifespan.

My children and I watched enormous pylons rise on the north side for the new bridge. Cranes, one on top of the other, were giant toys in Crayola-red, blue, and yellow. On-river construction sites floated like dystopian islands, with vehicles and tall stacks of beams, girders, and brightly colored shipping containers. Magnificent concrete and steel pieces were layered to form the bridge, and while fascinated by the engineering, we were wistful to see the old bridge and its homonymic name go. Sometimes, my teenage children indulged me with an ironic chorus of the Pete Seeger song.

The little lighthouse remained. It defied the suburbs and General Motors when they pushed the land to its stone base in the last century, although the beacon was eclipsed in 1965 by lights on the Tappan Zee. At the George Washington Bridge, Jeffrey's Hook Lighthouse was long ago enshrined in the book *The Little Red*

Lighthouse and the Great Gray Bridge (1942). That story was re-playing here at Tarrytown as the new bridge reared its concrete-scaled back, a hydra encroaching upon the white lighthouse.

February 2016, no holiday, no children in the car, just me hoping for light traffic as I drove north for my increasingly fre-quent visits to my aging parents. My thoughts on the bridge were crowded by anxiety as I planned a strategy for convincing my eighty-seven-year-old mother that she could no longer care for my ailing father alone.

On the way back, my eighteen-year-old son was with me, re-turning from a choir conference in Boston. He did the crossword puzzle on his phone, asking me for some answers. I asked him to tell me what he saw from the bridge. I wanted that skyline, hover-ing like the Emerald City, "closer and prettier than ever," to yield its promise of a new heart and maybe some courage.

"Yes, I can see the skyline," my son answered, "and a barge." He turned back to the puzzle.

The next month, I crossed the bridge, sad and alone, driving south from my father's funeral. Not even the radio, just the silent shell of my car, protecting me until I could scurry into the sanc-tuary of my house. I could not remember the drive north at all, only my children's singing and playing music to keep me focused on the road. We didn't talk; I'm sure I didn't glance around the bridge.

On the first span heading south, a phrase from a Hebrew song popped to mind—"narrow bridge"—from a saying attributed to the Hasidic Rabbi Nachman of Breslov: "The whole world is a very narrow bridge, but the main thing to recall is not to be afraid." Though the Tappan Zee was wide enough, my life felt shrunken, so I performed the quick ritual of taking in the pan-orama and, right away, I was on the down-sweep to the other side of the Hudson, to New Jersey, and Pennsylvania, and I coasted, the bridge carrying me with a fleeting sense of relief and solace, to the second half of the journey, away from my childhood town and my father's grave, toward home.

Note: When this essay was completed, the Tappan Zee was still intact. By publication, it was completely gone, replaced by the Governor Mario M. Cuomo Bridge, a soaring, white harp of a bridge that thrums when you cross it. Perhaps my children's children will someday hum along.

8

The Heron

RETURNING FROM MY SUMMER VACATION some years ago, I was greeted with an overripe flower arrangement on my doorstep, apparently delivered for my birthday a week before. The birthday itself was one of those whole numbers I would have preferred to forget, as I also wanted to forget the ex-lover who'd sent the flowers. He, however, seemed to have forgotten I'd be away on my birthday or that the romance was over. But no matter.

I was about to trash the whole thing but became morbidly fascinated with the stalks of lilies going limp, the carnations fading to a visceral pink, and the necks of daisies breaking on their own weight. Ferns shriveled. The petals of a mauve rose had begun to dry. A green florist's sponge, punctured by the cut tips of stems, came off in crumbling chunks. The moldering composition was contained in a blood-red metallic glass urn and smelled like last month's memorial service.

The arrangement sat on my bare dining room table, decomposing before my eyes. *Nature morte*. As the old masters would have understood, it was already dying the moment the florist created the arrangement. I enjoyed my sarcastic symbolism.

I really should throw it out, I told myself.

But something occurred to me that I could do with the flowers that might do me and maybe the universe some good. A mixture of rituals, albeit a bit off-season.

The month of Elul, preceding the Jewish New Year, would begin in a few days. During Elul, some reflect on shortcomings and mistakes of the previous year and ask people for forgiveness, and we are supposed to forgive others. The next month, Tishrei, signals the new year. For my purposes, the relevance was that the second afternoon of Rosh Hashanah, we throw breadcrumbs into a moving body of water, as if shedding the sins of the past year. The practice is called *tashlich* ("cast off"). This practice occurs before the communal confession of sins and request for God's forgiveness, on Yom Kippur (Day of Atonement).

I always loved tashlich, even though the concept of sin remained obscure. When the children were young, we'd collect ends of bread over weeks and freeze them. At the river in the park, the kids delighted in tossing the bread to ducks and geese, who snatched up our stale bread before it could float away. I'd ask the children to think of a regret or habit or secret that they wanted to throw away for the year. I suspect their sins were as slight as the tiny crumbs that dissolved and disappeared in the green water. In the little Mediterranean town where we had lived in France, we balanced on enormous boulders on the jetty (from the French jeté, "thrown") and tossed baguette ends into the waves.

Now, in the first few days of Elul, I would undertake a floral tashlich, although I wasn't completely sure whose sins I would be casting into my urban stream. In the recesses of resentment and pain, I knew we each bore responsibility for the eventual rotting state of our encounters, but I knew my plan might not yield forgiveness. Nevertheless, I needed to move on. This would be an amalgam of rituals though: instead of engaging in tashlich once, I would draw it out over seven days like a period of shivah, the week of mourning after a death, although I was past grief. Each day, I could pluck a piece of the arrangement, walk down to the footbridge, cast the shreds of organic stuff into the river and, with that, discard a particular piece of resentment or chagrin.

I began. Rather than pull out whole flowers, I decapitated some of them or plucked a few daisy petals so I'd have enough for the week. Perhaps this small violence was not in the soothing spirit of the original tashlich or the gentle grace of shivah, but this was my ritual.

As I denuded the arrangement over the week, it was transmogrified into a kind of ikebana—if ikebana had been assembled by Edward Gorey. Anthers and blackening leaves drifted from spent stems onto the table. There was a certain precision to my ritual. Like meticulously washing a body for burial or preparing oneself for mikveh, a ritual bath, I made sure to collect every hair's breadth of filament, every strand of fern that fell. Some days, I eschewed the flowers and just scooped up the day's botanical crumbs from the table as my offering. Making sure to get every grain of pollen reminded me of how we are instructed to collect each morsel of leavened bread, each crumb, as we clean the house before Passover. This cleansing washes the soul as well as the windowsills, yeast representing bloated sin or self-absorption. I was glad to weave these various practices and beliefs together.

When the vase was empty, I intended to clean it thoroughly and donate it to Goodwill.

The first day, I set out at sunrise with some trepidation and a fair amount of embarrassment, along with my small, sealed plastic bag of flower parts. I hoped to get to the river before the runners and dog walkers started their days.

On the steep path to the bridge, the forest smelled loamy and sweet, the scent of August that I associate with the turn of summer toward its end. Heavy rains had made the woods lush, but the path was clear. The last of the night insects sang. On the bridge, as planned, I looked only downstream, not up, leaned over the rail, and dropped two carnations into the water. They sat upright in the muddy stream, churned by the previous night's storm, and their stems glimmered beneath the surface. The pale pink flowers eddied toward the banks, and I was anxious that they might snag on a rock or be deposited in the mud; I really wanted to see them float down the river, out of sight, along with any shards of bitterness. They skirted a tree snag, floated languidly, and then stopped in a still pool. I watched, willing them to move. Soon, a slight current caught the flowers and swirled them around the bend of the river. I peered until I couldn't see them anymore, feeling some measure of relief.

By the time I climbed back up the path, the cicadas had begun their chorus, signaling a hot day.

One day, down the hill to the river, the mist was rising, and in sight of the bridge, sun cast rays through the trees. Glinting in the fractured morning light, perhaps thirty-five feet above, an enormous, perfectly round spider web spanned the path.

Another day, as I watched petals, stems, and sepals disappear down river, I noticed a family of mallards all in a row, preening on the far bank. Indifferent to my ritual, they picked at their feathers with their beaks. The iridescent blue of their underwings caught the morning light.

Other days, I looked forward to seeing the spider web, if the light was right. I watched the various ways the flower parts traveled—some halted by a rock, some sank, some were born swiftly on the main current, others turned and bobbed and lazily followed the twists of the riverbank. One morning, I brushed yellow pollen off my hands, and it glistened as it fell before dispersing over the water.

Sometimes, I questioned the point of it. The week felt longer than seven days, and some mornings, I felt an old surge of resentment or sadness, wanted another ten minutes of sleep. But I did it anyway. Ritual is like that: you repeat it, and remain open to rare glimpses of transcendence or grace.

Some pieces of flowers sank right away. I peered into the dark water to see them glow, fade to the bottom, and disappear. Rust-colored petals of alstroemeria bobbed in the river in a light rain, tiny boats bearing away my worn-out hopes. There was a beauty to it, poignancy. I felt lighter walking back up the hill to home and breakfast.

On day four, I added to the ritual. I turned to the other side of the bridge and looked upstream, but not until I'd completely unburdened myself of the day's spent flowers and moribund memories. Not until the stuff disappeared downstream.

A slimy, torn-up lily was my cache for the day. Some of it sank, some floated, but a stem snagged on a branch near the bank. The stream rhythmically tugged but failed to loosen it. I waited. I needed to make sure everything floated away, not stay stuck, as I'd felt stuck. I stopped myself from turning upstream and instead hurled hot streaks of vengeful fantasy after the lily. The stem still held fast to the branch. I felt both ridiculous and close to tears. I waited.

After another couple of minutes, a slight breeze stirred the water, and the stem drifted away and disappeared.

Turning to rest my arms on the rail on the upstream side of the bridge, I watched the river rush and burble over rocks, bringing fresh water from its source. Its source? The Source? A word some use for God. Really, I told myself, this was drowning the metaphor. But why not? Especially since I stood in the middle of a bridge, trying to divest myself of pain and start fresh, these flights of fancy were appropriate. Bridges, in Judaism and other traditions, have deep symbolic meaning, and I found myself humming a melody about bridges.

Those first few days, my ritual was to package up the flowers and, on the way to the bridge, decide on a particular image, event, or feeling to discard. I would meditate on the departing flowers until they disappeared along with their accompanying memory or regret, however long it took. Then I could enjoy looking upstream.

But I started to get impatient, more eager to look upstream than to lob cynicism and stinky flowers downstream, more excited to see what the river would bring for the future than to spend my time urging on the drifting past.

In fact, especially if it hadn't rained, the water appeared still in the downstream direction; petals could sit and rotate in place for quite a while until an eddy pushed them forward. I not only wanted to get the ritual over with or at least make it more efficient while keeping it meaningful, but I also needed to get home and to work. On day five, I didn't wait to see if the flowers made it round the bend. I'd let go of them, and even if they caught on a branch or rock, I imagined that a storm would probably loosen it all, sending it downstream.

Bad habits being what they are, even after I'd created some measure of serenity in my daily walk and ritual, I couldn't help myself. That lovely image of a storm washing away the little memorial bouquets and their sins was disturbed by an image of my former lover, downstream, maybe noticing bright petals in the water and wondering where they came from, catching a mysterious shiver of something important. But no. That was stale romanticism on my part. Who would notice tiny flowers in a big river?

I shook out the last little stems, along with the nostalgia, and quickly turned from the drifting flowers.

Upstream, away from the quickening current near the bridge, the same mallards put in an appearance, bobbing in a quiet pool near the banks, flipping upside down to feed in that comic way they do.

Day six, my penultimate day, was already hot even though it was early and clouded over. Mosquitoes and gnats swarmed my head on the hike down, and thunder rumbled across the valley. I flipped some flowers downstream, muttered less than a reverential prayer, and turned away to regard the river coming toward me from upstream. A bit mesmerized, I stayed too long. It was muggy. The runners were arriving. I was tired and itchy climbing the hill.

But it rained lightly on the way home, cooling my sweaty face.

Day seven, the last, I woke happy, looking forward to something, not sure what. It was earlier than usual, quiet, no one on the path. With each step on the way to the river, I recited my version of the Yom Kippur confessional, things to do with participating in a distorted relationship, not assuming enough or the right kind of responsibility, hurting myself by remaining too long, maybe forgiving too much, asking not enough.

I looked for the spider web, but the sun wasn't up to illuminate it. When I reached the bridge though, a thrilling sight met me: a great blue heron stood in the water upstream where I wasn't "permitted" to look until I'd emptied my burden. I quickly dumped the remaining flowers into the water downstream, stuffed the plastic bag in my pocket, watched the flowers for a second, and turned to the other side of the bridge where the water rushed from its source.

I was afraid I'd startled the heron, but there it was upriver, standing in the shallows, spreading and folding its wings.

I've always loved herons for their mystery, their smoky blue color and their great wingspan that you see when they take off low across a river or lake. I love their unmistakable, hunched silhouette in the sky and their prehistoric enormity.

The heron lifted its feet and placed them deliberately, stalking a fish, drawing its head back, ready to dart its beak into the water. It drew back again, moved slowly toward the bridge, never taking its eyes off the water. I could see the details of its feathery head, long beak, and the gray-blue of its wing.

Although I'd seen herons flying in the area, I'd never seen one this close on this river. I couldn't help thinking that this was it, this was why I did this, though maybe I didn't know at the start:

to note what's gone, but only briefly, and to leave the past in its murky doldrums and not check to see what happens to the remains, the memento mori of a dead relationship, and, instead, to be surprised, excited about the future, to look upstream to what is coming down the river toward where I stand on the bridge.

The heron shot its head forward into the water and emerged with a large fish, shook it, raised its head, and gulped. I watched it feed and then take off with a haunting glide, back upriver.

Before heading home, I glanced once more downstream. Some of the rose petals I'd thrown that morning had landed on the riverbank. Maybe they would decompose here, feeding local flora to bloom next summer. Or maybe, when the river rose again in a thunderstorm, the petals would make it downstream. Even if they didn't, maybe some tiny molecules of the decomposed flowers would travel down the river, through the city, to the ocean, and, borne by strong currents, mingle with all our faded cast-off bouquets and dreams. And the next time I visited the Atlantic coast, I would swim in the nourishing, complicated sea.

9

Polonius and the Jabberwock

WHEN MY YOUNGER CHILD WAS SIXTEEN, we decided to memorize Lewis Carroll's "Jabberwocky," from *Alice in Wonderland*. Chrys loved the performing arts, so their desire to learn poems seemed natural. Less expected was their interest in doing that with me. I was thrilled, but you can't reveal that to a teenager.

We quizzed each other on lines, practiced dramatic delivery, debated pronunciation of *"mome raths,"* gave each other notes like stage directors do, and laughed at the double entendre we evoked through tone of voice. Soon, we planned a public recitation for extended family.

I am no actor. In fact, performing scares me. Besides a few bit parts in high school, I've always preferred watching plays or reading them. Except for reciting La Fontaine's "Le Corbeau et le Renard" in ninth-grade French class, I've rarely done more than read poetry to myself, which I truly enjoy. In any case, this was Chrys's project, and they were a willing, poised performer so would go solo.

After Thanksgiving dinner that fall, in front of fifteen family members, Chrys took a breath and, in a mix of whimsy and threat, began, "'Twas brillig, and the slithy tove." Their voice became an eerie song at "all mimsey were the borogoves," and perky with, "as in uffish thought he stood." Chrys recited, pulling us into the story as the boy in the poem, with "vorpal blade" in hand, commenced the battle with the Jabberwock. At the final stanza, Chrys growled, "And the mome raths outgrabe," and took a melodramatic bow.

We knew "Jabberwocky" from bedtime stories, and it was full of inventions like "snicker-snack," which smacks of speedy destruction but also something tasty while sounding like the poet is winking at his own seriousness. Commonly labeled "nonsense verse" and relegated to collections of "children's best-loved poems," it had always seemed one of Carroll's quirky concoctions that echoed fairy-tales and myths but mostly it was just a charming trifle. In learning the poem and in the hubbub of our family Thanksgiving, I didn't mark any significance besides a fun challenge we'd shared. So, I was surprised when days after Chrys's recitation, a line reverberated in my memory.

"Come to my arms, my beamish boy!"

I began to think the choice was not coincidental and that there might be something more to our pastime. Warning of dangers, the father in the poem sends his child alone to fight a monster, and the unnamed son returns, with the Jabberwock's head, to his father's welcoming arms. It seemed more than nonsense, more than a paternalistic test of "manhood," as I'd sometimes conceived it.

Chrys was in the middle of those years when children change so quickly—their moods, their desires, their very selves dance and skitter and do flips beyond our reach. And I was in that phase of parenthood between doing and observing, helping and keeping one's mouth shut. I was feeling the starkness of this period and heard whispers of the threats that might become my own child's "bandersnatch." I could warn about "slithy toves" but knew my child must eventually contend with many of those alone.

In fact, Chrys had already navigated part of a new emotional landscape that was both challenging and inspiring. A few years prior, they'd declared their gender identity, anew, but this coincided with more painful events than any young teen should have to handle, so the early adjustment was burdened with anguish. Our family held hands through part of this shadowed place, but more than once, Chrys chose to approach the precipice and mountain alone, turning back only to stop their father and me from accompanying them. I knew there were more "mome raths" than were revealed to us, and I also knew the larger world contained threats. And tangled under all this was adolescence, ready to snare and trip up.

But, like the father in the poem, I could also rejoice. "Callooh! Callay!" the parent in the poem exalts at his reunion with the child. "Come to me," he says, and I heard in that invitation not only pride but also relief and the knowledge that the parent could not have accompanied the child.

But what of the child's perspective? I pondered that, which the poem didn't seem to. When the boy in "Jabberwocky" returns to his father's "chortle"—a joyful sound that perhaps veils relief and hope—maybe the boy is relieved as well. Or maybe, as he approaches his father, he fears being pulled backward, overshadowed, his own voice muffled in his father's embrace. Except his "uffish thought," we don't hear the boy's view at all: in his quest and return, does he feel terror, exhilaration, relief, pride, ambivalence? And if the child had chosen not to return that time, does he know the welcoming arms are there anyway, always? I wondered if the boy's awareness hovers around the father's pride and relief. Our study and recitation made me think about my own children's experiences with send-offs and homecomings, threats and triumphs.

"Jabberwocky" brought into relief that stage of life and relationship with my own child, the push-me-pull me quality of the adolescent years. But most of this philosophizing came later.

We next joined the witches 'round the cauldron in *Macbeth* (act 4, scene 1). In reciting the poem, Chrys gave the gruesome images a cast both evil and sardonic; the "hell-broths . . . thick and slab," the "tongue of dog," and even the "finger of birth-strangled babe" were delivered with bite and sly humor. Theirs was an in-your-face performance, again with family, and I was proud of this fiercely independent interpretation, this fiercely independent child.

I'd hoped we would continue our poetic studies together, but the sparkle of friends and activities outside home enticed Chrys more than some dusty verse with Mom. That was as it should be, and wistfully, I treasured the time we had spent with witches and monsters.

Poetry, though, was not absent from my life. Lesson plans for my college and medical school classes contained poems and plays, so I could enjoy returning to some of the familiar verses.

Soon after Chrys and I learned "Jabberwocky," I happened to assign Polonius's farewell speech to Laertes (*Hamlet*, act 1, scene 3) for one of my classes. I knew from experience that the scene was a good entrée to Shakespeare: some of the lines would be familiar to the class (e.g., "to thine own self be true"), and the rich imagery and word play would engage them. Inspired by learning the two poems with Chrys, I decided to privately memorize Polonius's monologue while teaching it.

Polonius is often played as a bumbling, garrulous old guy or as a ponderous pontificator, not someone students (or teenage children and their parents) necessarily identify with, but it's an appealing scene nevertheless. I'd read *Hamlet* several times, seen theatrical performances and movie versions, and stumbled on too many misty greeting cards and "motivational" posters based loosely on the text, so despite its pedagogical value, it had become almost a throw-away speech in my mind.

But once I started studying it on my own, along with hearing my class's interpretations and what caught their attention, for some reason, I noticed something new in the rhythms, puns, and images. Mostly literary insights, but other perspectives as well.

As Chrys and I had done, I tried out different voices—at first, self-consciously, even though I was alone in my home office, but soon I was bellowing out the lines, laughing at myself and ignoring my child's tolerant smirk when they happened on me practicing the verse. Studying it regularly meant the lines became an elegant "earworm," more often on my mind than the few minutes each day that I practiced. Reciting brought the scene alive; hearing my students' discussions and recitations refreshed it.

Having the words in my own mouth, I began to make the scene my own: to memorize, I had to get inside of the character. I started to feel the ebb and flow of emotion as if journeying with Polonius as he sends Laertes off. At that point, I was happy to play with the scene, and it was satisfying to learn the lines, but the meaning seemed the same as ever: advice to a son from a lofty father, like a Jabberwocky dad, only wordier and with a focus on a child's departure rather than his return. And again, the child is silent. But as I practiced and heard my voice, something else began to brew.

One day, I noticed that Polonius is nagging Laertes in the opening lines. He is basically saying, move your butt so you don't miss your boat, with the pun "you are stayed for" referring both to his hanging around too long and to the "stays" of the sails that are, by contrast, ready to go. Ironically, Polonius delays Laertes's departure with a protracted piece of advice (and just one more thing, son). Perhaps Laertes is muttering a Renaissance version of, "Yada, yada, yada."

Reading these opening lines one day, I grinned to myself, thinking, "It's like Noah." Earlier, my son had a reputation for getting ready at the last minute and forgetting things while the family packed the car or raced to catch a flight. Maybe Polonius and Laertes were closer to us than I realized.

I wasn't intentionally digging for meaning, but on another day, merely practicing the monologue, I recited the most familiar line for the hundredth time—"To thine own self be true"—and

something came into sharp relief. Over the years, I'd read *own self*
as if it were one word, evenly spoken as a tiny iamb that doesn't
merit embellishment, especially if you're reciting in that exag-
gerated way. ("To *thine* . . . own *self* . . . be *true*.") The phrase had
seemed obvious. But this time, I accented the word *own*—not
on purpose but because something welled in me, and those tiny
words flooded the poem with a new sensibility. I didn't know why
a change in emphasis revealed something. I sat there taking it in.

My voice caught on "own" and echoed with memories of my
own past choices along with hopes for my children's future.

I knew that poetry and plays may provide comfort, catharsis,
or insight, but looking closely at Polonius, at that phase of my
life with one child at home, the other at college, it struck me
hard: the character may be giving Laertes advice, but he's also
reminding himself of a sharp truth. Making impossible choices,
trying as we can, sometimes showing little for the effort, we learn
how hard it is to stay "true," but only later do we realize the poignancy of it. Of course, this was not the first time I'd contemplated regret, choice, the sense of straying from my "true" self
either because of necessity or trepidation, but I felt it in a new
way. While Polonius tells Laertes how to dress, handle money,
and judge friendships, he may seem verbose, but his words are
also imbued with fervent hopes for his child and thoughts of his
own past strivings, failures, regrets.

Another line in the opening, "The wind is in your sails," also
rang in a way it never had, echoing the goodbyes, the times I
launched my children to other cities, other countries, the next
phase of life. The unknown. Polonius is rushing Laertes off, but
he's the one who isn't quite ready.

The scene became a lens, magnifying my fears and hopes for
the children, and moreover, the scene highlighted complicated
feelings about my own past. When I spoke those words, I heard
not only Polonius's detailed advice, but like the father in "Jabberwocky," the vain desire to protect at a distance, the love threaded

with worry, and the sad knowledge that the child would likely struggle to remain true to self. My own past hovered in the wings while my children were beginning to take flight.

There was something else that intensified my identification with Polonius and prompted new revelations. Practicing alone in my home office one day, I suddenly noticed my own voice, and the obvious hit me: I am a soprano, I have a "female" voice. I identify as a woman. Abruptly, Polonius became a mother, and not only was a female Polonius an appealing dramatic option but also made me feel more fully the ubiquitous experience of children's departures and our own past departures from home and parents.

I hadn't marked the gender of the characters when I started rehearsing; it was just fun knowing those great lines. Of course, I knew that the gender of actors need not be consonant with the characters', but as an amateur who imagined Polonius as a mother—or a parent of any gender—I felt more embedded in the character and in the voice that spoke the heart-wrenching worries and hopes of all parents.

Later, I contended with Laertes's gender, too. What if it were a young woman or a nonbinary person? What if one kept the gender ambiguous? Would it allow us to identify more deeply with the characters, help us realize the itchy ambivalence of many departing children? Could we enliven the silent Laertes, just as we might the barely visible, unnamed son in Carroll's poem?

Noticing and shedding the specified genders infused the poems with power. It also made me start to think that I could draw a ritual from this practice of poetry.

Often read at weddings and funerals, poetry is powerful; in fact, I included poems in the programs for my children's b'nei mitzvah, ones that reflected something I saw in them at the time. But such readings are incidental; ordinarily, learning the poem isn't the ritual. In liturgy, however, we repeat prayers and psalms over time, and both are forms of poetry. Perhaps, as with prayer and other meditative acts, I could transcend the ordinary only after repeating and studying a poem or scene and, especially, learning it by heart, not just reading it once at a ceremony. Poetry and plays aren't meant to be read once. Whatever the writer's original intent, a good poem perturbs our souls and our memories in new ways over time, meaning changes, and like prayer, the act may change us, too. To yield the power of ritual, the piece might have to be examined and recited again and again.

So, maybe it took my actually studying, memorizing, and reciting these works over time to render them more than an academic exercise or a ceremonial ornament. Work and effort provided insights, as some rituals may do, and maybe it became part of my experience of the emerging changes in my children and me individually and in our relationships. I eventually came to see the Jabberwock and Polonius as more than capricious choices; instead, they were a chance for insight and a small part of a shift in the way I was being a parent.

There is a fine line between the therapeutic and the ritualistic, the psychological and the spiritual. Speaking and identifying aloud anguish, yearning, confusion, and change, whether in therapy or in prayer or poetry, may not prevent evil from finding us, but language is part of our armor. Representing our experience in poetry might ease a transition. A poem could be an incantation against pain and for joy, but whether it "functions" that way or not is beside the point: the act of studying the poem may render events more meaningful.

My child and I learned poems and scenes at a particular juncture, and I continued the practice solo. It may have drawn us together in those few, sweet hours, but there was a wonderful paradox. We were sharing something fun together—something more mature than the childhood craft projects with glue and beads and construction paper—yet the themes in "Jabberwocky" (and in the scene from *Hamlet* that I did alone) were those of leaving, of independence, of pulling apart, with all their complexity. So, poetic studies could have drawn us both together and apart. I sensed in these works a reflection of Chrys's stepping away to contend with life on their own; perhaps the poetry highlighted ambivalence about that.

It's possible I read too much into this and imposed a heavy importance on a fun pastime and an academic exercise. Was it co-incidental that the two pieces I spent the most time on were first, about greeting one's child after they battled a gnashing monster, and second, sending them overseas alone? Though sixteen-year-olds likely have more demons ahead, maybe, through poems, they (and their parents) can imagine those future threats and the ultimate departures that leave us parents behind and, perhaps, the family reunions. For me, the symbolism and identification were unavoidable. In the midst of that phase of life, the poems became a mirror.

While I was learning the *Hamlet* scene, a vivid memory from my childhood joined Laertes and Polonius on the dock. In the fourth grade, a poem first became more than a bunch of singsong lines. My teacher had given an open-ended assignment to choose a short poem, memorize it, and recite it to the class. I asked my mother for a suggestion, and running her fingertip over the po-etry collections in her study, she plucked an E. E. Cummings anthology off the shelf. "These are fun," she said, or something like that. I flipped through, looking for poems that were less than a page long, and arbitrarily chose one. I recall this event clearly because I later jotted it all in my juvenile diary with its lime-green patent leather cover and tiny lock and key.

That week, my mother and I sat on the screened-in porch sur-rounded by azaleas and dogwoods in bud outside, a hint of spring in the cool New England air. I'd recite lines, she'd correct me, encouraging some pauses and phrasing. At some point, the lines suddenly jumped out at me, and I felt something close to what people describe as revelation: "A blue true dream of sky . . . of love and wings . . . of the great happening illimitably earth." And the opening phrase, "i thank You God for most this amazing day," jolted me out of my listless study. For the first time, I had a sense, as if at the edge of my peripheral vision, of something beyond the tangible. So, this is what religious people were talking about! None of the Jewish prayers I'd had to learn, none of the rituals or holidays had done it. But there it was, the "illimitably earth" and the "blue true dream."

I told my mother. I probably said something like, "I think I believe in God; I think I understand what people mean." Although this belief was a transient one (for I was an avowed atheist), at that moment, I was excited to share my starry-eyed revelation.

I do not remember exactly what my mother said, but I know that in an embarrassed but gentle way, she made light of my emerging religious sensibility and likely returned to pointing out the naturalistic imagery and the rhythm of the poem.

Along with my spiritual revelation was one about parents: they can really get it wrong sometimes. Here was a moment like none I'd experienced, and I was a child looking for validation. Later, I realized that despite his stated agnosticism, I should have broached this with my father. Even though he was the science-trained physician and my mother, the humanities-trained language teacher, Dad had more tolerance for ambiguity. But Mom was doing the best she could, protecting me from the mushy dangers of spirituality.

And no matter. I'd seen the power of poetry, and if one has any religious or other kind of transcendent inclinations, those will emerge again. Much later, I saw in that poem, with its lowercase "i" and uppercase "You," echoes of Martin Buber's "I/Thou" and other meanings. The poem came to mind over the years, unbidden, and was a comfort, a paean to life.

Like my E. E. Cummings experience, learning poetry with Chrys and on my own was a serendipitous ritual. While I felt something in my relational landscape shift with Chrys, I am skeptical of deliberately creating a ritual based on literature. I suspect that many modern teens—and adults, too—might roll their eyes at the idea of learning poems or plays as a rite of passage or as a ritual to move through a difficult time. De novo rituals, especially ones that feel like school, can feel artificial; prescribing ritual may sap it of meaning.

Yet, in Chrys's and my poetic forays, there was one area that seemed ripe for deliberate ritual, a ritual that might be palatable to a young person (or a skeptical adult like me). I mentioned earlier that the child's point of view was absent in the poems we studied. Perhaps one could imagine and write or, better, improvise the child's response to the Jabberwock dad and to Polonius. We could ask, "What would *you* say, my beamish child, my stayed-for child?"

I do not know if that act would be therapeutic or ritualistic or educational. Maybe it doesn't matter.

At the least, we could create the conditions for ritual in poetry. When my undergraduate students studied literature, especially poetry and theatrical scenes, we were not engaging in a ritual, but I believe there was an emotional—perhaps even spiritual—benefit for us all. They delved into the language, the structure, and themes. They read the work aloud, sometimes memorized it, and they wrote poetry and scenes, too. But in focusing on the literature itself, personal dimensions rose naturally; a seemingly academic analysis sometimes yielded an unanticipated emotional shift, an insight.

With my medical students, studying and writing poems and scenes not only served psychological needs but also seemed to provide a ritualized bridge to new stages of professional identity. The poetry was perhaps a rite or incantation to drive away the goblins of loss, worry, and fatigue that haunted their training and professional work. Yet the ritual was never overt; I never said, here's a ritual for you, and I only became aware of the ritual possibilities as they happened or after the fact.

The lines between art, ritual, and psychology have always been blurry; some ancient theater traditions arose from religious practice, and "catharsis" in theater originally referred to purification. Perhaps we could reconstruct poetry's old purposes for modern sensibilities. And yet, part of the reason my medical students' poetic study glimmered with ritual was because we hadn't marked it as such. Instead, we were faintly aware of ritual possibilities. Paradoxically, just studying the poems but with an eye to a different plane of experience made it more than academic. Perhaps we could do the same with children or by ourselves.

I've emphasized the *act* of studying poetry as a potential ritual, but can we deliberately select poetic themes that will serve ritual as well? It was only in retrospect that I realized the relevance of Chrys and my poetic choices to that stage of our lives. And I'm not sure that we could have made a deliberate effort to choose "relevant" poems. How would we know? Their development and our relationship were, as always, in flux. Moreover, it was the implicit and unexpected themes that were the most powerful. Imagine saying, "Let's have fun finding poems about adolescence! Identity formation!" *Cringe-worthy* is the word that comes to mind. Like the indirect, serendipitous benefits of poetic study in my classrooms, perhaps the themes need to be stumbled upon, too.

Yet I did select particular poems for my medical students that contained themes relevant to their current experience: "uncertainty and choice," "evil and sorrow," "felicity and humor," "relationships." At the same time, I included few pieces that directly dealt with medicine, hospitals, or illness. I didn't need to; unprompted, they brought those experiences to the table.

As for the poetic forays with my child and by myself, if there was a ritual quality to those, I can only say that it was there for me, not necessarily for Chrys. I wouldn't presume to impose that on their experience and memory. In time, they would create their own ways to leave, to face the dark woods, and to be true-to-self—and, maybe, to come galumphing back.

10

Tamagotchi and the Dodo

ONE ICY WINTER DAY, when the children were ten and thirteen, they returned from school to find their beloved guinea pig, Hershel, had died. Six years seemed to me a short time to have a pet, but evidently, it's a respectable lifespan for a guinea pig. Besides, the cocoa-colored, busy little guy, with his musical squeak, was their first pet and had accompanied Chrys and Noah through much of their childhoods, so they were sad to lose him. He'd been named for a deer in an Isaac Bashevis Singer story we happened to be reading during the winter holiday when he arrived. The children were delighted at a name that means "deer" in Yiddish and that both the fictitious animal and their pet were brown. I think they also enjoyed adults' bemused reactions when first hearing the name "Hershel" attached—not to someone's great uncle or a Talmudic scholar—but to a cilantro- and strawberry-chomping rodent who enjoyed scurrying through a PVC-pipe maze in the dining room.

Soon after he died, the little pet's corpse was interred with a ceremony in the garden, next to the cherry tree. We wrapped him in a cloth, placed him in a shoebox, and the children added his favorite bell toy and other accoutrements. They each scattered a trowel full of dirt onto the cardboard coffin, per Jewish tradition, and we stood in silence, per Quaker tradition. If memory serves, each of us shared a story or attribute of Hershel.

Sad as it perhaps was for the children, the death of their pet had plenty of precedent for devising a funeral, some of it quite ancient. Not so for a series of losses my son had experienced earlier in childhood.

As a preschooler, Noah liked to visit the Academy of Sciences in Philadelphia, where we lived. At the time, something he called the "roaring dinosaur" greeted visitors inside the 19th Street entrance. This primitive animatronic device swayed and bellowed and terrified him, so we'd rush past to spend the morning in the hall of gemstones; in the live butterfly room where cecropia moths and monarchs flitted and landed on us; and in the hall of dinosaurs, where the models and skeletons stayed put, and the only sound was the laughter and chatter of families. Noah spent a lot of time chipping away at a pretend paleontology dig and liked to perch on the bronze, life-size sculpture of a Galapagos tortoise.

He was the kind of child who liked his adult to read every museum label, including the scientific names in Latin, which he'd repeat over and over. We'd look at dioramas of taxidermy animals, and he'd ask about ones he didn't recognize. Although petrified by the roaring dinosaur, he loved to handle live millipedes or snakes that attendants in the hands-on children's exhibits offered. Perhaps the uncanny nature of the fake brontosaurus was too creepy; a real arthropod or reptile moving of its own accord delighted him. In the woods near our house, we had to teach him early not to pick up random spiders or touch poisonous leaves and mushrooms, all of which fascinated him. Nature seemed central to who this little boy was.

One day, on our way to one of his favorite exhibits, a room of constructed animal habitats where children could climb inside logs or view an active beehive, he asked to be lifted so he could see the paintings and drawings that lined the hall to our destination. I thought nothing of it at first; he'd never seemed to notice them before, perhaps because they weren't three-dimensional, so they were maybe less intriguing to a preschooler. I picked him up to show him the illustration of the passenger pigeon and dutifully read the label. He furrowed his brow in what I assumed was his usual concentration, taking in the details of the pigeon's history and its coloration, and pronouncing the rhythmic name, *ectopistes migratorius*. We moved to the next picture, a dodo. I read the label, and he plopped onto the floor, crying, "Why did they do that? How could the dodo be *gone*? And the pigeon."

He'd seen an illustration of a dodo in his *Alice in Wonderland* book, but that was a fanciful story, so perhaps he thought they were make-believe. However, he did not know about extinction.

I hadn't protected my children from the realities of nature. In fact, Noah would carefully collect dead cicadas on our porch, saying they would be food for birds. And though he was sad if we found a dead fledgling bird, for example, a simple explanation of the inevitability—or evolutionary necessity, a concept that intrigued him later—seemed to console him. But extinction? None left? Forever? I hadn't anticipated his reaction.

Once his crying stopped, he demanded to know what else was extinct. I mentioned a few but didn't inform him of the rate at which the insects were disappearing, never mind the charismatic mega-vertebrates or the glaciers and rain forests.

A packet of tissues, a hug, and an ice cream mostly restored him. But I knew he'd left the Garden, and I wasn't sure I'd handled it all that well.

Is there a ritual for mourning the extinction of a species? My imagination failed me. In fact, I confess I was just glad to have it behind us, at least at the time.

To be sad about an extinct species is perhaps similar to mourning the death of a fictional character. It requires imagination and some abstract thinking and deep empathy, I suppose.

But I never thought a palm-sized chunk of plastic filled with electronics would be worthy of mourning.

When he was a tot, Noah received a hand-me-down toy from his cousins, a "Tamagotchi," a little plastic creature that used the primitive electronics of the time to show when it needed food, sleep, nurturing. Noah tended it for a while, but seemed to be getting anxious or bored or both. "Do I have to keep taking care of it," he asked. "No," I replied, "we can just put it in the closet." He was several steps ahead of me. "But what will happen to it? Will it die?" I didn't want to crush his childish imagination, but I also didn't want him feeling like a murderer or neglectful care-taker. Like the roaring dinosaur, this little object resided in the "uncanny valley," that psychological place of neither living nor inanimate.

I explained that in the pretend, electronic world, yes, it would stop working, but no one real was dying. My handling of this incident was as inadequate as with the dodo. He was deer-in-the-headlights more worried and ambivalent than ever but agreed to put it in the closet. I think he sneaked a peak now and then. Perhaps the batteries ran down. I don't know. But the thing did "die" from neglect. I trust we recycled it responsibly.

I should have helped him create a ritual, like we eventually did when the guinea pig died. Mourning the Tamagotchi required some of the same emotional capacities that the dodo's absence did. What was missing was a ritual.

But it wasn't only extinct animals and electronic toys that re-quired our mournful attention.

A large sugar maple bloomed at the corner of our property. The tree provided shade in the late afternoon and a brilliant orange, red, green, and yellow rainbow in the fall, and when the leaves fell, we'd rake them into an enormous pile to jump into. But the emerald ash borer had apparently invaded sugar maples in the Northeast and, making its way south, had attacked our tree. It had to come down.

Still very young, Noah was bereft. "Can't we give it something like medicine?" he said. "Why does it have to be cut down?"

The day the arborists came, he sat on the floor of the playroom, alternatively stopping his ears with his fingers to muffle the sound of the chainsaw and adding to his worlds-within-worlds of miniature trains, Legos, and Tinker Toys.

But the thing about maples is that their seeds sprout easily. We used to spend some portion of our gardening energy in the spring pulling up shoots from the tulip and iris beds. The children liked to collect the seed pods, drop them from the porch, and watch them helicopter to the ground. Or even more satisfying, they'd carefully peel back the edges and stick the perky, green pods on their noses or foreheads like a miniature beak or unicorn horn. They never tired of this.

Walking out to the garden after the tree guys had left, we took in the fresh smell of the sawdust, the stump cut flat to the ground. We tried to count the rings in the stump to estimate the age of the tree. Then Noah noticed that several maple sprouts, maybe three inches high, surrounded the area. "Can we water them and grow a new tree?" he asked.

Apparently, when a tree is dying it may shed extra seeds, perhaps to ensure its genetic legacy. We had our pick of sprouts near the original stump. Noah selected the one nearest the original.

Two decades later, it's about thirty feet high, though the fall color is more yellow and brown than the brilliant colors of an average sugar maple. Perhaps its offshoots didn't breed true; perhaps the pest persisted and marred the normal changes in chlorophyll. But it is, nevertheless, a full-grown offspring of the original.

This wasn't the only time a tree caused him to mourn. One day, inside the house, we heard a deafening crack from the street. We ran outside to a surreal scene. An enormous tree across the street had split at its base and lay like a great, beached whale, reaching the width of the street and onto our sidewalk. Neighbors congregated, walked the length of the tree. Its girth was astonishing, nearly my height of just over five feet, something we hadn't realized in looking at it when vertical. Many of us instinctively ran our hands along the bark, marveling at this mammoth.

It took several hours for a city crew to come and cut up and cart away the tree. But Noah was worried about something. "Where will Pooh Bear live?" he asked.

Years before, the tree had begun wearing away near the base, the bark and cambium eroding to form a hollow cave in the wood, maybe two feet high. Our neighbors had placed a Winnie the Pooh stuffed animal inside, with a hand-painted sign just above, saying "Pooh's House." Neighborhood children occasionally left cookies, honey, or tiny toys for Pooh, who apparently appreciated these tributes, for they stayed only briefly at the entrance to his home.

After the city workers had cleared the enormous trunk, branches, and debris, we saw that they had left the base of the trunk with the little cave; the tree had apparently broken above it. For several years, Pooh's house, repaired after the accident, remained until one summer when the neighbors took out the stump and replaced it with a fig tree, perhaps a fitting tribute to the previous tree, and with wonderful connotations besides: "Everyone shall sit under their own vine and under their own fig tree and no one shall make them afraid."

But these arboreal losses proved tame compared to what happened on the way to a High Holiday service one autumn in the early 2000s.

At the time, our synagogue couldn't accommodate the Rosh Hashanah crowd, so they rented a large hall twenty minutes or so from my house. The driving route passed farmland, sheep and goats, copses of trees silhouetted on a hill, a white clapboard barn with green shutters. Noah peered out the window and hummed to himself as we made our way back and forth during the holidays.

That autumn, we headed off on our pastoral drive. When he first glimpsed the sheep, he exclaimed, "But what's that?" In the distance, trucks hauled building materials, and bulldozers gashed the land. A pile of felled trees and a wide slash of dirt signaled that a road would be built right through the old farm. I slowed enough to see a construction sign with a rendering of the condos that would spring up in the next several months, like an invasive fungus.

I was silent for a minute, hoping he wouldn't realize what was going on.

"They're digging up the field!" he cried. "Why are they doing that?" He kicked the back of my seat. "What about the bunnies?"

Rabbits were special to my son, and he knew that rabbit warrens might run underground in fields and near hedges and forests like these. I could only say they were building apartments.

He was silent for the rest of the drive. Every time we passed the area, I also had a sinking feeling. In a Faustian deal, the farm trust had apparently sold some of the land to support the rest of the trust.

Perhaps it was my limits as a parent, or maybe it was one of the times that I let my own feelings overwhelm my ability to comfort my child. It twisted my stomach to see the construction going up but, more so, to hear my son's cry of anguish for the irrevocable loss.

What is the memorial prayer we should chant for the loss of a tree? For a beloved swath of field or forest? How do we memorialize an extinct species? I recall my anguish when I returned one autumn to my childhood home, built near watershed land that included the woods where I'd played as a child. At the reservoir near our house that Thanksgiving weekend, I came upon a clearcut of trees. Granted, this was far from old-growth forest; it was, in fact, neat rows of pines planted, I assume, to control erosion. But the pine forest had been old enough that it supported wildlife and the imagination of a child who loved to tromp on the soft pine needles, catch toads, and float miniature canoes she'd made of white pine bark down the small creeks that ran from the reservoir.

So, I understood my son's sorrow but had no spiritual remedy.

In later years, some of his work reflected a commitment to environmental concerns. But I still wonder if we could have done something different, something that acknowledged the profound nature of those early losses, that honored the fall of a tree, the unknown cry of the dodo.

11

On the Playground

SOME OF US HAVE THE LUXURY of choosing when our children realize the existence of violence. We live in neighborhoods without gunfire and have excellent health care; we are surrounded by greenery and innocence. We decide when they first learn about war, violent prejudice, and the murder of children who live on blocks we rarely visit.

September 11, 2001, tested this privilege and my ability to make meaning of the events.

That morning, my three-year-old, my three-month-old, and I headed to the public playground, a ten-minute walk if you're on your own, twenty or so if you are pushing a stroller and holding the hand of a toddler. At the park, I swayed the little one in the bucket swing. The older one pumped his legs on the big-boy swing, higher and higher, singing a little tune over and over under the crayon-blue sky.

Often, I made small talk with other parents or met a friend, grateful for the adult company. In our neighborhood, we lingered on the playground to exchange tips and news and perhaps something more intellectually stimulating than "Thomas the Tank." But that day, the playground was empty under the blue dome of sky.

Few people had mobile phones then, so I approached someone walking across the playground. I must have said something like, "It's quiet. Where is everyone?" "You haven't heard," she replied and told me. I instinctively looked up. Not a plane, not a traffic helicopter. Nothing except the stark blue sky.

I couldn't catch my breath. I quickly bundled my infant into the stroller, took my son's hand. Time to go, I must have said, though we'd likely been there less than a half hour.

I have no memory of the walk home except when we passed the elementary school. I was terrified to see that the children were playing as blithely as ever; they hadn't been sent home yet. I kept repeating to myself, "I have to get home. I have to get home," as if this mantra could keep all the children safe. Like a rabbit racing to its burrow, I was desperate to put my children down for their naps. I kept thinking that if I could get the little one into the crib, the bigger one in his bed with the protective sleep rail and his stuffed bunny tucked securely in his arms, they would be safe, away from the intense blue sky.

My son's window shades were printed with a dreamy tableau of fields, streams, bluebirds, red-and-white polka-dot mushrooms, and gentle clouds; my baby's curtains had fanciful giraffes, deer, and horses surrounded by trellises of leaves and flowers. I closed the shades, shielding them from the shocking blue sky.

I raced up the stairs to call their father and turn on the television. Despite my horror, I couldn't stop watching the scenes in New York, at the Pentagon, and in the Pennsylvania countryside, barely three and a half hours from my house. Switching among channels, I saw the same unreal destruction over and over. I kept the volume low so the children wouldn't wake up. I glanced at the frozen blue sky.

I didn't want the children to wake up. I wanted them to sleep a long, long time. I wanted my children to remain suspended in their sweet dreams. Maybe they could fall into a long sleep like the princess until the barbed, choking vines were cleared. I didn't want them to wake up, because when they did, I would have to compose my face and body to hide my shock and terror and somehow stop the horror from seeping into their dreams. When they did wake—and still these decades later I don't understand why I thought this—those televised scenes would be realized. It was the very mundane nature of our lives that scared me. In the World Trade Center, mundane life had been going on: people doing business, having a pleasant lunch, flirting with a colleague, avoiding a boring task, mopping the floor of the bathroom. When they did wake, I would have to resume our normal life and open their shades to the painful blue sky.

It happened that an older friend from abroad was in town and came to lunch some time that week. We talked about the attacks. She shrugged. "What do you expect? They're terrorists," she said, as if explaining how my family should deal with this. As one who'd lived through war in her home country, she was, if not blasé, then certainly not panicked. On some level, I understood, but when I said that I wanted to prevent my son from hearing about it—this little boy for whom the scariest thing so far was probably the winged monkeys in *The Wizard of Oz* movie—she said, "He's got to learn about the world sometime. It's reality." And she shrugged again, that shrug that signals *I've seen it all; this is life.*

But I would not tell him. I would not let my son see this yet.

Vigilant when the TV was on those following weeks, I somehow managed to keep the images out of his sight, signaling family and friends if they seemed to start to talk about it with him present, so I was fairly sure he had not learned anything about September 11 that fall. But over time, there were hints that I may not have been successful, though I wasn't sure. And I don't remember when and how we told him later. It's possible I simply copped out and let the thoughtful, responsible professionals at the children's schools in later years help both of them comprehend and commemorate 9/11 in an "age-appropriate" way.

I was no better, though, at comprehending and commemorating the event for myself. Indeed, I am ashamed that throughout the years I did nothing special on the anniversary except for shedding a guilty tear as I listened to public radio broadcasts on that day.

The year 2021 felt different. It felt important to commemorate the twentieth anniversary of 9/11. Maybe it was the current state of the world or just the gravity of two decades having passed and demarcating a generation. At some point, my younger child had ruefully noted that their birth year would always be easy for people to remember: Chrys's age was the duration of time since 9/11.

The twentieth anniversary also coincided with the advent of the High Holidays, early that year relative to the secular calendar. Perhaps this added to my emotional state, with its defenses already worn thin by a violently divided political landscape and the sense of urgency to do something to acknowledge the day.

As sometimes happens, I began to obsess about what I would do for a ritual I didn't yet have.

The website for the memorial site at Shanksville, Pennsylvania, depicted an appealing, pastoral place where a memorial was scheduled for the eleventh, but I didn't feel like going to a commemoration with strangers, many of whom would likely be survivors or families of survivors. Even though it was open to the public, it felt as though I'd be intruding on an intimate, painful event. I didn't want to be a tourist at such a wrenching moment. I did intend to visit the site at some point to leave a memorial stone or flower, but not on that day. The events near my home were unappealing, the slate of speakers filled with personages likely to pontificate rather than create a sacred space. I wondered if I should go to DC or New York, but I didn't feel like being in a crowd, maybe filled with people snapping selfies in front of the 9/11 memorials, something that seemed obscene.

Maybe I should just watch the memorials on TV or listen to the radio, I thought. Maybe go to synagogue that morning (it would be a Saturday). But I honestly did not feel like dealing with the rigmarole of services. And I didn't want to be in a crowd I didn't know in another city or neighborhood, but I didn't want to be alone. Nothing seemed right. I needed something simple, something meaningful, something that permitted contemplation without corniness, community without crowds.

The night before, I still hadn't figured out a plan. But something fluttered at the edges of my awareness.

That morning was as clear and beautiful as the day twenty years before. I woke early. Wind had swept away the humidity and the clouds. Birds lingered in the garden despite the crisp air.

My neighborhood was still. I walked up the gentle slope of the street near my house. No traffic yet, just the occasional neighbor walking a dog or jogging.

When I reached the playground, I realized I hadn't walked into the park in a few years, though I drove by it all the time. The entrance was different from two decades before. A wooden gate and pergola adorned the pedestrian entrance, and leafy shade trees, planted in the intervening years, had grown to maturity and lined a new path. Though there were some new play structures, many of them were the same, and I imagined my children in the past at different ages on the slides and climbing bars, increasing the height and daring of their exploits over the years, balancing on the top, dangling from a hoop, gliding across the track ride, and heedlessly leaping from swings at the top of the arc. They would ask me to make up an obstacle course and time them as they raced through it. I remembered my younger one on the tire swing, asking to be pushed faster and faster, and hand-over-hand, swinging along the monkey bars smoothly and without hesitation. Even the bucket swings my little ones had enjoyed were still there.

I strolled slowly through the playground and noticed the tiny wooden playhouse with its various climbing structures. A faint patina of moss had softened the rough wood over twenty years.

It was silent, just after eight in the morning, and as two decades before, the park was empty.

When I neared the playhouse, I teared up. Perhaps it was remembering Chrys as a very young child lolling—there is no other word for it—on top of the monkey bars, as if it were the most natural thing in the world. Comfortable at heights, graceful, they experimented with the apparatus.

But I was not here for nostalgia, surprised and touched as I was by the rush of vivid memories. At that moment, the full force of the day came to me. I sat on the bench for a minute to reflect.

Sometimes what one is supposed to do arrives unexpectedly, naturally and unplanned.

I didn't think of it, didn't expect it, didn't say, okay, now do this thing. It just came. A whisper from my lips.

"*Shma* . . ." I began. "Listen."

I stood at the bench looking at an empty playhouse in front of the woods, and the "Shma" and the "*V'ahavtah*" (and you shall love), the brief, two most important prayers in Judaism, came from my mouth.

Tears streamed, and I thought of nothing, just sensed without words the sadness and loss and passage of time, and accepted that a prayer had washed over me, someone who doesn't pray.

The short prayer finished itself. It was around eight thirty in the morning.

As I was finishing my unplanned ritual and feeling a clean wash of serenity, my tender reflections were interrupted by loud exhortations, a shouting group, all accompanied by throbbing bass notes and thumping electronics.

My usual reaction would be to get annoyed—how could anyone be playing loud music and shouting on this quiet, sacred morning?

But I felt curious rather than irritated, amused rather than indignant. Walking to the public tennis court, I took in the scene. Garbed in brightly colored leggings and tees, a large circle of mostly women were doing calisthenics and jogging in circles in time to a compelling musical beat and the ringing encouragement of a smiling exercise leader. Some were singing along to the music. I had the impression they did this every Saturday. I sat on a bench and watched them for a while, impressed with the energy and camaraderie, the laughter and the singing.

It was, in a way, a service, though the participants hadn't intended that. It was as moving as my small prayer, maybe more so, since the sharp pain of the day was complicated by joy. The humanity of that exercise class, the very optimism expressed in the songs and shouts and movement—the very normality of it—seemed a perfect ritual to honor the day. This was a way to commemorate: to jump and lift weights and skip and laugh and play raucous music. This was one way to defy incomprehensible cruelty and violence: we are here now, we are unconstrained, we dance and shout our joy and freedom under a gorgeous blue sky.

12

Sacred Pages

AT THE END OF THE TEACHING TERM one winter, a frenzy
of grading, meetings, and frantic students sent my culinary habits into a nosedive. The fridge and freezer contained half a limp
cabbage, frozen lumps that were probably ground turkey or beef,
a handful of pathetic carrots, last week's desiccated rice, and containers of leftovers I was afraid to open. I peered at it all, hoping
for something to gel for my Friday night dinner.

A possibility emerged: a delectable, perfect mouth-feel comfort food that isn't fussy. All I had to buy was ginger snaps.

I dug through a frayed manila folder containing dozens of
torn, stained papers, some over forty years old, and found a small,
pink telephone memo sheet from the days prior to voice- and
email. Scrawled in my hand was "G'ma Rose's Stuffed Cabbage"
along with notes from my maternal grandmother, Belle, and from
"Nicki (VT)"—all variations on a theme of cabbage and ground
meat, cooked forever.

So much information on this tiny paper: ingredients; instructions; and, in some cryptic orthography along the edges, my
mother's advice not to bother stuffing the cabbage but just make
meatballs, roughly chop the cabbage, and throw it all in a pot.
Belle indicates "sour salt," sugar, and tomato sauce, while Rose

orders lemon juice and ginger snaps. I preferred the latter because the cookies thicken the sauce and imbue the sweet-sour blend with an elusive spice.

I thawed some meat, kneaded it with the leftover rice and an egg, and prepared my misshapen sloppy version of Grandma's snug rolls. It's tricky; the cabbage breaks, the meat oozes out, and the recommended stove-top cooking is also hard: keep it simmering without sticking to the bottom or burning and without the cabbage rolls unrolling when you stir them.

A tiny note at the bottom of the page stirred a memory. I'm standing in my shiny kitchen in a brand-new ranch house, in a brand-new marriage, in rural Pennsylvania, asking my grandmother over the phone what she thought of ground turkey instead of beef and getting her advice about the cabbage breaking when you roll it. I could almost hear her ironic frown over the phone at the very notion of turkey. The note about the cabbage says, "Boil it almost done first."

But why keep these hastily copied recipes, stuffed into the folder over the years? It would be easier to have them typed up and organized since I do use some regularly, and the annotations would be easier to read.

I keep the stained, pink scrap of paper because it is sacred. I keep the folder of scraps because they are part of a ritual.

Along with the memo sheet, the folder contains "From the Desk of . . ." pages; backs of receipts, torn-off corners of magazines, a crumpled paper that simply reads, "Dorothy says add a quarter grated onion to latkes [potato pancakes]"; and, thanks to my Great-Aunt Ruth, there are three sheets of Royal Viking cruise-line stationery with her "kuchen" and several chicken recipes. Whatever was closest to my landline or to the chef's elbow in their kitchen is what I, or the cook, wrote on. Most are in my own handwriting, but sometimes, an old typewriter font or my mother's Palmer Method handwriting, or her mother's, which was nearly identical and like my mother's, became smaller and shakier in the same way as they each aged, decades apart. A simple recipe for scones from my friend Nat is in elegant pen-and ink calligraphy on fine paper, too beautifully rendered to be placed on the counter and stained with batter. A postcard from our family friend Joyce: "Thought you might enjoy this recipe from Finland," and a neatly printed index card from my Aunt Shelley delineates a satisfying, "Sunday Night Pasta" with spinach-cheese sauce, from our early days of vegetarian cooking.

On a torn corner from the paperback cover of the *Moosewood Cookbook* (1977) is "Mom's Perfect Rice" (one-and-a-half-to-one ratio of water to rice, cook from cold, covered, don't stir, fifteen-minutes total from cold to done). It is, in fact, perfect. She learned to cook rice in Japan, when my parents lived in Kyushu after my father served as a medical officer in the Korean War. I'd copied this recipe into the cookbook so I wouldn't lose it, probably the year I got that first cookbook and my first apartment. The cover fell off, so I tucked the rice recipe into the file.

There are multiple copies of my children's preferred birthday cakes because when they were young, I was too rushed to find the one in the folder, so I would just call my mother to dictate it to me again over the phone, then I'd cram the extra copy into the folder before cleaning up the sticky remnants of batter and frosting and candy decorations. My younger child preferred the chocolate (as did I as a child), the older, vanilla (as did my middle sister), so the recipes are respectively labeled "Wendy's Birthday Cake" and "Laurie's Birthday Cake," just as my mother titled them in pen on the pages of the *Betty Crocker's Picture Cook Book* (second edition, 1956) from which these recipes derived.

In the folder are my crude diagrams for the children's "shape cakes," also inspired by my mother's practice. She made us turtles and swimming pools and the quintessential 1960s "doll cake" that had an actual Barbie doll stuck in the middle of a poufy, frosted and candied cake dress emanating from her wasp waist. Somewhere in the folder is a small *Baker's Coconut Animal Cut-Up*

Cakes (1959), a pamphlet put out by General Foods—I assume it came free with the can of Angel Flake Coconut advertised on the back of the booklet. My mother, and in later decades, I used the ideas as templates for our early attempts, but we went well beyond the blocky, midcentury "hobby horse cake," "Perry the Penguin," and "Myrtle and Milton Mouse" (one assumes they were avoiding copyright challenges) illustrated in the pamphlet.

Leafing through the recipes forms a sacred ritual, in part, because it evokes layers of memory. The notes for children's birthday cakes makes me feel the weight of that *Betty Crocker's* with its frayed binding. As a child, I climbed on a chair to reach the cookbook from a high shelf in my mother's kitchen. Its illustrations are in colors that can only be from the 1950s; smears of chocolate and spots of vanilla extract baptized the recipes, marking the years. I loved looking at the photos of the perfect cakes. Years later, the cakes I made for my children weren't perfect, but I loved carving and decorating them, making magic with candy and frosting.

I like remembering my failures, too: a full-sized, round basketball in chocolate cake that deflated overnight or the enormous cake in the shape of a car key, made the year my son was eligible to get his license. At that party, the group of sixteen-year-old guests took one look and laughed; my children grinned at me, raising eyebrows at what they apparently perceived as a phallus. In my defense, the silvery frosting had softened the crisp lines of the key that I'd carefully carved in the dense vanilla cake.

Sifting through my file of recipes evokes swift streams of time, the flurry of boots and backpacks jumbled in the front hall, rafts of blocks and crayons, double helixes of carpools, cheerfully chaotic birthday parties, and the quick runs back and forth to the car for the homemade Thanksgiving cranberry bread or Passover almond cake for holidays at the grandparents.

Even the recipes I've never made became sacred: "Chocolate Pancakes," from a woman whose daughter shared the school bus stop with my children. By the time I considered trying the recipe, one of my children was already in college, the other, not often home for Sunday morning pancakes. But reading it, I remember those sweet, hectic days of waiting, craning our necks for the bus, talking about our children and our lives.

Another recipe I'll probably never make—"Mary's Samosas"—with paper-thin crust and labor-intensive filling. Seeing the recipe, I fantasize the aromatic spices, the kick of hot peppers, crisp dough giving way to al dente diced vegetables. I keep it and recall Thanksgiving dinners at my childhood home when Mary, a family friend, and her husband brought samosas as appetizers. We'd sit in the living room, dipping samosas in a sweet-hot chutney, the flaky filo dough drifting onto our laps. The year after she and her husband retired to Santa Fe, she mailed a frozen batch to our house.

In turning over the pages and making some of the dishes, I remember particular periods of my life: "Dave's chicken" recalls disorganized communal dinners with friends the year we graduated from college, and "Laurie's Chicken Curry" brings back my sister, tan and lean, returning from a bike trip in the 1970s. "Mom's Meatloaf" evokes the ultimate comfort, with its ketchup-brown-sugar glaze, but with my penciled amendments of sunflower seeds, cumin, and currants. After a particularly rough patch in the early 2000s, "Chicken with Pears" became one of my signature autumn dishes. Reading it, I feel the tug of love and loss, but grief transforms to celebration through the alchemy of cooking this dish for friends.

Also in my file are long shopping and logistics lists for "Noah's Birthday 2003," with notes to "buy pomegranates and starfruit"; "Rosh Hashanah 1999," and also "tenure dinner," "mitzvah, Friday night dinner" ("candy-coated fennel seeds, gold chrysanthemums, purple table cloths"), and a recipe for "Halloween Eyeballs" involving marshmallow and peanut butter.

I keep this haphazard collection not only to remember events and periods of time but also people. Reading my mother's note on her brisket recipe, "always chill overnight, skim fat from sauce, slice very thin . . . to get the most mileage out of it," I am at her side, watching her trim the Rosh Hashanah roast with surgical precision. When small chunks fell off, we ate them while we plated the rest, even if it was eight in the morning. As I read, I recall her holiday shopping and organizational charts, her aprons and her seventies coiffure.

There's a card with a bean soup recipe penciled with my notes at odd angles ("add thyme, rosemary, a smoked turkey leg"), which became my "Sukkot Soup." Looking at it, I not only taste the smokiness of the turkey and the richness of the beans but also remember a chilly October evening in our outdoor sukkah (booth) adorned with pine boughs, gourds, and apples. My neighbors came for dinner in the sukkah and brought their son, daughter-in-law, and infant grandson. I look at that recipe and see our little boys stuffed into their snowsuits in highchairs, their cheeks pink in the chill. After the grandparents left, the trio stayed way past sunset; the couple became two of my best friends. Our boys became close friends, too.

In addition to evoking memories, there's another reason for maintaining this ritual of paging through and sometimes cooking. Many of the cooks who gave me these recipes are gone, and the majority of them were women. These sacred pages are part of their legacy; the words are poetry, the product, artistry. So, the stuffed cabbage recipe with the verbatim quote from Grandma is one of the few links to her and to my father's family. Murmuring her words and making her cabbage rolls is a sacred act. "Rosie's (aka Rose) Rolled Cake," typed by my father's brother on the occasion of my grandmother's funeral, is also in the file. Uncle Bert is gone now, too, and so, reading his typed recipe for his mother's famous confection evokes not only her hand and voice ("refrigerate dough . . . roll it all up . . . bake until done"), but also my uncle's humor: "Guarantee [he wrote]: If you follow the directions it will never come out the way she made it . . . Rosie never used a measuring cup, had an old aluminum scoop, and a 'handful' was certainly a variable." And even though I've never attempted the chewy-crunchy texture and tart-sweet perfection of "Grandma Belle's Candied Citrus Peel," just looking at that recipe, cradled among the various layers of life in stained pages, conjures my maternal grandmother's quavering voice singing the 1941 "Tying Apples on a Lilac Tree."

Some of these recipes I took down verbatim as I stood next to these women. "You have to smoosh it like this," my grandmother said, and I wrote her words on the recipe as she kneaded the cookie dough. In an elegant Dallas kitchen, I scribed every word my great aunt uttered in her gravely, smoker's voice: "Here's how much brown sugar." Her chunky rings shone under a patina of flour.

Some I've never made. "Mrs. Kolodney's Orange Fluff Cake," courtesy of Grandma Rose. Maybe Mrs. K. was a neighbor in Grandma's Brooklyn apartment. Perhaps they shared their recipes, a friendship. I leave my measuring spoons in the drawer and imagine them in their housecoats and sturdy oxfords, peering at me and proffering tiny mounds of powdered sugar in their cupped palms. I'll probably never render poultry fat for my Grandma Rose's "Chopped Chicken Liver" recipe, but the tangible, ritualistic act of paging through my precious parchments renders a rich sense of continuity, identity, and meaning.

Paging through, reading, and cooking these women's recipes, I embody their memories.

The week before Rosh Hashanah one year, I looked for a traditional honey cake recipe in one of my Jewish cookbooks. None of them appealed to me: too many nuts and raisins. Then I remembered the cake my friend Lois brought decades before to my tiny apartment on Green Street. It was a hot day. I had no air conditioning, and as a first-time holiday host, I'd ambitiously and foolishly roasted an enormous turkey, which sat enrobed in towels because it was done too early. Lois's family and I crammed around my maternal grandmother's old rickety kitchen table, sweated, and ate turkey and honey cake.

I rifled through my overflowing folder. There, in Lois's neat script, was "Mrs. Lichtenfeld's Honey Cake." No idea who Mrs. L. was. I made the honey cake, and it was as if Lois was with me, telling me it was okay that the flour didn't dissolve completely in the batter. Honey cake, yes, and also many late afternoons at her kitchen table over tea and a cookie, talking, commiserating, laughing.

Lois was a painter and a magnificent sculptor who avoided the stress of mounting art shows, preferring instead to immerse herself in her studio, a continual installation of *assemblages* and magic. She had enormous blue eyes, full lips always coated with bright red lipstick, a shock of short white hair, and a laugh ringing with mischief. We'd comb the city for objects for her sculptures. At a particularly low point in my graduate student career, on one of our jaunts, we entered a tiny south Philly shop and she urged me to try on an emerald green, sequined minidress and stiletto heels. She caught my eye in the mirror. "I know you," she said nodding, "A lot more is going to happen. You are not done."

I make the honey cake and think of that dress, of Lois's voice and laughter. Of what she was trying to tell me. She was thirty years older than me and a dear friend. I touch her notes and conjure her fears and her audacity. She became part of my own sense of self. When I make "Mrs. Lichtenfeld's" honey cake, Lois and Mrs. L. are immortalized. And I—the least mystical of people—feel their presence hovering over the rich brown batter and the smell of allspice and cinnamon.

These recipes are little *megillot* (sacred story scrolls), preserving my foremothers' stories and my own. They comprise a sacred ritual because they preserve the memory of ancestors, particularly the women and what they left for us, and because they link their interpretations with mine. The notes in my mother's hand for how much wine and matzah to buy for Passover; the purple beet and golden turmeric stains on puckered pages of my borsht recipe; the notes upon notes all signal celebration, sorrow, and remembrance. Like all good rituals, we make these recipes over and over.

Of course, religions have used food in formal rituals; for example, at the Passover seder, one "tastes" the bitterness of slavery in a sliver of raw horseradish and the "bread of poverty" in a sheet of matzah; the Muslim *suhur* and iftar meals bookend each day of fasting during Ramadan; and the Christian sacrament of Eucharist is signified by bread and wine. But I am talking about something apart from religious practice: using a humble recipe folder and its contents, which hold glimmers of the sacred. And the process of paging through and cooking these recipes is an effective and sacred ritual partly because it is inefficient and impractical.

Yes, inefficient and impractical, like many rituals. Not only the "wasted time" of having to look through the myriad recipes but also the nature of these recipes: they are often inexact and so vague as to be poetic.

One may never get it exactly right since those old recipes require cooking without precise measurements and directions. It is this very lack of precision that prompts concentration, as when one is fully engaged in a traditional ritual. The necessity of *re-creating*—not following—produces engagement, not rote. In this musing, meditative state, I not only recall the women who passed these recipes on, I also enact their legacy and summon their voices, hands, and the smells of their kitchens; I embody something fundamental. The very elusiveness requires not only cooking experience but also a kind of shamanistic practice. And if we repeat this creative, sacred act over time, transcendence is possible. We reconstruct and perhaps add to suit our tastes, but we preserve the essence of the recipe and our ancestors.

Contending with the ambiguity, figuring out quantities and proportions of ingredients, is more akin to Kabbalistic study than to culinary science or art. To ask what a "medium" potato is now, relative to the 1960s, or how much is "enough butter to dot the kugel [noodle pudding]," or what is intended by "till done," prompts us to create not just a tasty dish but also to seek and create meaning. I read and reread the recipes, trying to discern the intent of the shimmering space within the letters. Sometimes, I telephone my siblings or children, inviting their commentary for my cooking Talmud. This also re-creates, conjures, and honors.

As I tinker with salt, sugar, the balance of butter to flour, it is not precision I seek but sometimes the taste of times past. My foremothers whisper. This is an active process that imbues the moment (and perhaps the food) with magic, and it reminds us of who we are.

Seeking the taste of childhood is like tuning a string instrument; one feels it in one's sinews and inner ear. Like when the "A" is on pitch, when the sugar-to-lemon ratio is right, when the cake is dense enough to carve into a Raggedy Ann shape but not too fudgy, and it tastes like that green-frosted, turtle-shaped cake from childhood—it is right. When the pugachel (Hungarian cookies) taste as if I am in my grandmother's kitchen in the Bronx in the 1960s or the *charoset* tastes like I'm at a Passover table on an early April day in New England or when it feels like I am in that long-gone Boston apartment, trying to impress that long-gone boyfriend with my first attempt at guacamole, then I have it right. Whether the origins of the recipes were bitter or sweet, this ritual, like many good rituals, renews and restores.

But this is more than a Proustian experience because I experience this not only once and not only as a sense memory. Each time I attempt to re-create a sensation from kitchens past or, moreover, re-create a recipe I've never even tasted, I create meaning. The very repetition of paging through the recipe folder and its crumbling inhabitants—even when I'm not cooking— especially pages from those who left little else as legacy—the women—becomes akin to liturgy and ritual.

Seeking the taste of childhood. This happened especially one time I determined to make my grandmother's sugar cookies for my father's seventieth birthday. First, I bought an attractive tin to house my gift. This was the easy part.

Sugar cookies. If you're thinking delicate, cream-colored, melt-in-your-mouth wafers, think again. These are hefty, caramel-brown, sandy disks that stand up well to a long dunk in milk or coffee. They were christened "hockey pucks" by my brother-in-law. Grandma Rose called them simply "cookies" and dusted them with just the right balance of cinnamon to sugar, adding to the sweetness and loud crunch. Sometimes she made them fancy: a single peanut M&M was pressed into each one.

The dough was tough to work. I made the mistake the first time of trying to use an electric mixer; the potion immobilized the beaters. As I'd recorded on the recipe, there was, apparently, no cutting corners: I had to use my hands, as Grandma had said, feeling for the right balance of fat to flour, tasting or smelling the dough for the correct amount of sugar. Then, calibrating the knife-edge cooking time to get that dark brown but not burned look, the almost dry but not sawdust, crisp texture. And at what temperature? What kind of stove had she used? This part of the story was gone.

I tasted the first batch. Close: the flavor was correct, but the texture, too cakey. I tried again, consulting Tim, my husband at the time, who knew a lot about cooking. The second batch was closer: crisp, just the right cinnamon-sugar taste, right brown-but-not-burnt color. But still too moist. The cookies were supposed to be dry, and my family liked them that way. Was it the cooling process? The storage? The kind of fat? The pan? This was exegesis at its most challenging.

I made several more half batches. Each time we tasted the cookies, I'd have to describe to Tim what was wrong, since he'd never had the originals. We'd discuss what to alter. And this was a twenty-four-hour process because one had to refrigerate the dough overnight before cutting it in slices to bake.

Finally, after about five batches, the cookies were good: a bit dry, a pleasing brown; sweet, but not overly so, and a close-enough crumb. My father said, "This is the closest to the cookies I've had since Grandma made them." High praise indeed, but clearly, something in the way my grandmother "smooshed" the dough had gone with her.

Our legacy, our liturgy. I suspect that many women of my generation have a folder of tattered recipes tucked into boxes in attics or basements. In fact, Radcliffe's Schlesinger Library has dignified this practice with its hundred-thousand-plus cookbook collection and its scholarship on old, homely recipes. But I wonder how long it will last. Do grandmothers give their children recipes anymore, when you can Google "Jewish-style stuffed cabbage"?

If the folders no longer exist, then perhaps honorary appendixes remain in the form of our old cookbooks. Despite the apparent exactness of these published recipes, some of mine have become as much part of the ritual as their hand-crafted cousins. My spattered *Joy of Cooking* (sixth edition, 1975), the granddaughter of my mother's 1951, fourth edition, for example. My version still had recipes for tuna noodle casserole and baked potatoes ("snug in their jackets"). When I learned that later editions dropped some of the starchy recipes that used efficient "secrets" like canned cream of mushroom soup, I was kind of sad. I also have the 1964 *Sisterhood Cookbook* from my childhood synagogue. "Sisterhoods" aren't socially kosher anymore; they're called women's or members' clubs now. But here it all is, from Jell-O molds to *mandelbrot* to Ritz Cracker-coated chicken. And the best recipes in the world for hamantaschen (triangular pastries for Purim) and noodle pudding. Each year, additional pages become unmoored from the plastic spiral binding and fall like leaves.

In the margins of these cookbook recipes are layer on layer of notes, making them more akin to the ones in my folder than to precise culinary instructions. The magical dough in the hamantaschen recipe, courtesy of my sister's late mother-in-law, Lil, was too sticky to handle if you followed the recipe as published. When I called Lil the first time I made them, she said, "Add a lot more flour as you go, chill, and remove only small amounts at a time to roll out for each batch," the goal being to create the thinnest, crispest crust, with a high ratio of filling to cookie. I wrote all that down. (My family snubbed cakey hamantaschen with only a dot of filling.)

As with the folder, I page through these worn cookbooks, daydreaming and musing, not looking for a practical midweek meal, but imminence.

There is, though, one kind of cookbook that is not in my kitchen but sits on a living room shelf with Jewish texts. It is a book I will never use. Breast of goose, plum strudel, and other delicacies are described, along with recipes like "War Dessert" that substitutes margarine for butter, and others that note "eggs" in parentheses, as if optional. *In Memory's Kitchen* (1996), is an account of how a handbound collection—created and literally buried in the Terezín concentration camp during the Holocaust—made its way to the recipe collector's daughter, herself a survivor. These recipes are filled with memory, hope, and defiance.

I read with reverence; it would be blasphemous to crack the book open on my kitchen counter and make "Mrs. Weil's Soufflé" for dinner. I read and am a witness. I read and honor these women. The collection prompts a sacred moment, profound in a different way from my own ritualized recipe files. In all our tattered collections, we hear the whispers of all our foremothers.

In recent decades, my folder has welcomed something new: printouts from online recipes. For a long time, I resisted this, more inclined to consult my old cookbooks if I didn't have a recipe. Although neither as charming nor as sensory, some of the printouts have become part of my ritual, but I'm a bit sorry to see the scrawled ones become crowded by eight by eleven paper from my printer. Recently, after admiring a close friend's chicken that I'd enjoyed with his family on a Sunday evening in February, I asked for the recipe. He sent an attachment from *Cooking Light* magazine, which I printed it out. Not that I blame him; nobody handwrites anymore, particularly if it's from a cookbook or a magazine that's online anyway. But where were his commentaries? He's a good cook, so I know he didn't follow exact instructions. I should have done it the old-fashioned way: called and took his dictation over the phone.

When I use online recipes, I often print them out: at least actual paper will get anointed with spattered olive oil and my notes. This is not nostalgia nor a Luddite tendency; I just want to have something that's both lasting and amendable. Of course, online recipes are useful when you need exact measurements quickly. And yes, electronic "comments" accompanying webpage recipes are sometimes helpful. But those comments are from strangers, and though a detailed video of exactly how to add flour to thicken an asparagus soup may make it easier for me to make a midweek dinner, deciphering the hieroglyphics of "half a yahrzeit cup of sugar" or "whatever stale bread you have lying around" provides an opportunity to draw not only a meal but meaning from the pages. (A yahrzeit cup is a small glass, like a votive candle holder, for a memorial.)

I wonder if recipes being online in the twenty-first century dims the sense memories of an occasion. It's not in a familiar person's voice or hand, and we're likely to use it only once. By contrast, among my scripted folios is a bread recipe from a friend named Jane whom I met after college. We'd worked on a research project together, with a rather erratic boss. But Jane was ever calm; you could only tell she was irked by a slight tightening of her soft voice. She made a bread that I admired when I was at her apartment once, and in the same meticulous hand that had tallied data, she wrote out the recipe on one of those lined, three-by-five recipe cards, with a little illustration of a pot-bellied stove and flowers at the top, and a space for "from the kitchen of . . . ," "ingredients," and "recipe." Had the internet or smartphones existed and she'd sent the recipe electronically, I somehow doubt I would remember her voice, her kitchen, and our professional antics as clearly.

I admit, there are splendid online sources: worth a look is a YouTube video of a foolproof way to remove fruit from a pomegranate shell without white pith and without missing a drupelet. You score, split, and pummel half the shell with the back of a large spoon, and the fruit rains through your fingers into a bowl. I've watched that guy ten times. And it works.

Over the years, I've thought about retyping my recipes or putting them in a proper binder. Several acquaintances have self-published facsimiles of family recipes. I admire this effort but haven't been inclined to do that. However, when my younger child, Chrys, graduated from high school and got their first apartment, I assembled a collection of recipes that I'd solicited from extended family, typed up, and nestled into plastic sleeves in a three-ring binder. It included tips in each cook's voice. From Chrys's older brother, in a recipe for dhal: "lentils should be mushy, no crunch anywhere, but shouldn't be watery either . . . all spices are to taste: measurements are only suggestions." And in cousin Philip's contribution, "The L.R.W. Method" ("leftovers to rice to wrap"), in which most ingredients and many steps are parenthetically labeled "optional," he notes, "This isn't a recipe but a technique . . . a way of life even . . . to take leftovers and make it into two new meals . . . you have leftover-leftovers . . . and salt is a magical thing, but soy sauce is way more fun because it makes a satisfying sizzle sound in the pan." Perhaps Chrys would someday pull these recipes out of the protective sleeves and annotate them, add new ones obtained over the phone or in person, or scribble them onto the backs of used envelopes or lined notebook paper with scruffy edges left on, ignore my neat setup, and stuff the scraps into the file hither-thither. Create their own ritual. But that's my fantasy, not theirs.

In Jewish tradition, if a sacred text like a Torah scroll becomes stained or torn beyond repair, it must be buried with ceremony. For me, stains and rips on the sacred pages of recipe files are commentary rather than desecration, but if a recipe file is to be discarded, I wish it were done with some ritual. In early 2021, I came upon an old note to "ask Mom for her recipe file," but it was too late. Several years prior, she stopped organizing the holidays, stopped cooking anything more elaborate than a can of soup; dementia had eroded her ability to decode a recipe or execute it. During her move to assisted living in 2018, in the cleanout at my childhood home, her sacred cooking pages were whisked into the trash, and Mom's tattered file of recipes and holiday to-do lists are likely scattered in a landfill somewhere, along with "Anna's Spaghetti Sauce."

As for my recipe file, perhaps my children will sift through it when I'm gone, cook some, add their fingerprints and notes to the smeared sheets, stuff new recipes in, decipher the Kabbalistic message to "add much more water than indicated." But I know that legacy for one generation can be a burden to the next. But if they don't keep or use it, maybe they'll sift through it and sense the happy, cooking ghosts of their ancestors.

13

Coconuts

IN LATE JANUARY OR EARLY FEBRUARY during my childhood, our Sunday school teachers handed out something called *bokser* that they assured us was edible. When you shook the large brown pods, seeds rattled, and the stringy husks caught in our baby teeth. In 1960s Connecticut, it was usually a snowy day, so my friends and I were skeptical of celebrating this Jewish "New Year of the Trees" (*Tu b'Shevat*), when trees were supposedly blooming far away in "The Holy Land." As puzzling, the bokser alone seemed to be the entire holiday.

I learned later that the stringy pod was carob. It was probably picked months earlier, and slow shipment ensured that, by the time we gnawed on it, the bokser tasted like cracked leather and sawdust with a hint of ancient, bitter cocoa.

I also learned later that Tu b'Shevat was one of four "new year" feast days in the Jewish lunar calendar. Ancient tradition forbade eating tree fruit until the plant was four years old, so the full moon that coincided with the first budding trees would annually mark the age of a new tree. But observance withered over the centuries, along with the agricultural roots of Judaism.

Having only the memory of bokser to mark the holiday, I had little interest until my son was born, as it turned out, on the fifteenth of the month of Shevat, Tu b'Shevat. I was charmed by the coincidence. Maybe we could celebrate two birthdays, a Jewish and a secular one.

Over the years, we improvised a Tu b'Shevat holiday with friends, centered on a ritual dinner. My culinary goal was for each course to contain a tree fruit in some form, plus raw, whole fruits for ritual eating.

A cornucopia was the centerpiece. We shared each fruit, accompanied by blessings, interspersed with dinner courses and readings about trees. Inspired by old custom, a fruit with a hard shell, like walnuts, began the ceremony; then a species with a rind (kumquats, oranges); next, a fruit with inedible pits like dates, plums, cherries, or olives; and finally, fruits with fully edible seeds and skin, such as figs or berries. I liked using unusual fruits such as persimmons and starfruit, and we also included maple-flavored foods, since sap is part of a tree, and we loved maple-sugar candy. Per tradition, we also drank four different wines during the meal: white, then white with a drop of red, red with a drop of white, and finally red, representing the four seasons.

When we first started, there were few guides, so we created a booklet and, every year, added more tree-themed poems, songs, and stories. The pages reflected various times in the children's lives: a simple song about Torah as the "tree of life," which they belted out while clapping and marching around the table; poems by Edna St. Vincent Millay, Howard Nemerov, and Marge Piercy; psalms about trees. The pages also garnered splatters of pomegranate and papaya over the years.

It was a tasty if haphazard affair.

Years after my childhood encounters with the shoe-leather bokser, I took my then twelve-year-old and nine-year-old to Israel. It was December but warm enough to picnic with my cousin Terry at a national park. Scattered on the ground were dozens of enormous brown carob pods. We dusted some off and took a bite. Much fresher than the ones from my childhood: not quite juicy but getting there; still chewy, but easier to eat; and a rich flavor reminiscent of dates and chocolate. The children ran around the carob trees, jumped off picnic tables, and chewed on bokser.

The mystics who revived the ancient holiday in the sixteenth century would have approved: they believed chewing carob would ensure renewal of the universe. We have thirty-two teeth; God is mentioned thirty-two times in Genesis; we are to chew thirty-two times. They also thought trees were a metaphor for God's relationship with humans and the fruits were "emanations" of holiness, so they observed the day by ceremonially eating the biblical seven species to imbue themselves with holy intentions. Global practices varied over time. In India, Jews ate fifty species, and Persian Jews lowered empty baskets into their neighbors' chimneys to receive a full basket of fruit in return. Some of these traditions have been revived, and it also became customary to plant trees on the holiday.

In the days before Tu b'Shevat, my children checked the growing pile of fruit on the sideboard to make sure I was including their favorites, especially a whole, fresh coconut, which became our tradition for the fruit with an inedible shell. The children sat on the floor, placed the coconut on some newspaper, pounded a nail into the divots in the shell, poured out the "milk" and tasted it, and then gleefully smashed the coconut to bits with a hammer. An adult helped until they were old enough to do it themselves without pounding a sibling's thumb by mistake. As their dexterity improved, so did their messy exuberance and hilarity.

So, what were we tasting in the fruits of Tu b'Shevat? Since fruit holds the seeds of the next generation, medieval mystics thought that, by eating it, they helped God renew nature and fill themselves with holiness. Modern interpretations range from environmental awareness to reconstructed Kabbalistic views.

I do love the idea that biting into a kiwi might invoke a mystical, elusive aura from our ancestors or some kind of holy emanation. And something tasty that reminds us to repair our planet is welcome at the table. But for me, additional meaning is infused in the taste of those fruits.

The first year my son was at college, I found carob pods online and sent a package to him. The minimum purchase was far more bokser than anyone—even a gang of first-year college students—could consume. But he thanked me and, apparently, during his early years away from home, put together a Tu b'Shevat meal. I've never asked him what he "tasted" when he shared the carob with friends. Perhaps it was the taste of childhood, a taste as simple as chocolate, or perhaps something more complex, like persimmons.

Given my son's personality, I expect that humor might be part of the answer, too. A photograph from my children's early life shows them sprawled on the dining room floor. They're probably eight and eleven. My son clutches an awl against the coconut, with hammer raised higher than necessary, and a demonic expression on his face. Chrys is laughing, looking at their brother with delight, admiration, and conspiratorial glee (let's see if we can get Mom to remind us to be careful). The humor is not incidental to the ceremony and had become, like all meaningful rituals, repeated and perhaps necessary. Maybe the mystics laughed, too, when they broke open a stubborn shell of a tree fruit.

As our guests and I watched the children pulverize a coconut, spilling as much milk as they sipped and sharing the sweet fruit, what were we tasting? In part, we were simply enjoying a fun, sensory holiday that celebrated the cycle of the seasons and our ties to nature. Perhaps the experience linked the secular to the religious through the coincidence of Noah's birthday, and maybe, the spiritual to the environmental, or prayer to poetry.

Or, the meaning was elsewhere, in the actual taste of carob or kumquat, coconut or candied orange peel.

These are rare flavors for most of us, so maybe we tasted the ephemeral nature of gathering together, sharing a festive meal, creating meaning together over time. Perhaps the taste of these fruits not only evoked transcendent experience or environmental concern but also highlighted the precious time we had with family and friends. Maybe eating passionfruit or baking carob chip cookies reminded us to value time and life itself, as many rituals do. Could smashing a coconut once a year help us cherish those close to us and act on behalf of those distant from us?

The coconut may also have signified my children's devotion to each other. The taste of coconut pried from its impervious shell is like the inside jokes and the private stories they shared. A rough shell protects an essence that is sweet, unique, playful, and ephemeral.

In the days when the children lived at home, I loved preparing elaborate holidays like Tu b'Shevat. I relished hunting for hard-to-find foods, cooking, discovering new poems, setting the table, and juggling a meal and a ritual with a full table of guests. But after the children left, I sometimes felt unmotivated or at a loss; it seemed daunting to create the festival.

Was it only that I needed to adjust to the empty nest and a new phase of life? Perhaps. Of course, there is loss when children leave, but I was surprised by how much I yearned for these shared rituals. I started to think that trying to duplicate holidays from the past might not be sufficient, that new observances might be necessary. In fact, Tu b'Shevat had always been, for us, an improvised work in progress, and a disorganized one besides.

In winter 2022, I paged through our old homemade booklet with its numerous, lively, stained early entries, sparser additions in the later years. A simple illustration on the cover caught my attention. It is a rudimentary line drawing of a silhouetted tree with branches, trunk, and roots. For over two decades, I had seen the drawing, but that late winter, I noticed something: more than the trunk or branches, the roots caught my attention.

Trees had figured in my children's play during all seasons. In the fall, they liked to collect acorns and pinecones. Their piles of botanical debris accumulated alongside rocks, shells, and dried-out beetles. Sometimes they made collages or fairy houses or arranged their collections on the front steps. In September, they'd pick apples for Rosh Hashanah (the "real" new year). In November, they raked heaps of dry maple and oak leaves to jump into or throw at each other. In January, they touched the sticky sap seeping from the Norway maple next to the driveway. In the spring, the children stood under cherry trees as pink blossoms drifted around them. In summer, they climbed the Japanese maple at the front step, venturing further and further onto thinner and thinner branches as they grew bolder with the years.

Maybe playing with trees enhanced the children's sense of wonder and curiosity. Maybe it was just fun. In his early twenties though, my son shifted his gaze to a subtle aspect of trees: the lowly mushrooms, easily overlooked. He started to photograph, collect, and cook increasingly exotic fungi that grew near or on trees. He learned about species and processes that exist out of view: not only mushrooms but also the underground streams of nutrition and communication in the fungal web among the tree roots that help trees live. Beneath the ground flow warnings and opportunities, healing substances, competitive chemical weapons, and mutual aid.

Mycelium, hyphae, mycorrhizal. The terms for these hidden aspects of fungi ring like incantations.

Perhaps Noah's interest in mushrooms was part of an enduring ecological concern, but mostly, I imagine it was fun to ingest mushrooms and to tromp around and notice weird fungi or come upon ones that hid under rotting tree limbs. He exchanged photos in friendly competition with acquaintances.

My son's mycological enthusiasm might have drawn my attention to the roots in our Tu b'Shevat illustration, but the drawing prompted me to refresh the ritual.

Bare branches against the sky in February are beautiful, but the world beneath the trees is amazing. The image of branching roots, which literally and symbolically reflects the hidden below the visible, mirrors the tree above, and deserves a celebration. As an adult in the second half of life, maybe it was too simplistic to eat only fruit as if it existed de novo.

The old mystics might have agreed. They arranged Kabbalistic letters to form a tree, with all the parts corresponding to the "holy emanations" from God's source of life. While their tree of life was a metaphor for something beyond the material world, why not imitate the mystics, but with a modern sensibility: pay attention to the whole tree, with its invisible mycelial webs—and visible fungi? Perhaps the living things that we sometimes trod on have their own holy aspect or, at least, provide symbols to enhance our ceremony. I could acknowledge my son's birthday and the holiday in a new way, maybe add a mushroom course to the meal.

I wasn't able to gather with others to celebrate the year that I noticed the simple drawing in our booklet; instead, I went out under the Tu b'Shevat full moon, inhaled the cold, late January air, and contemplated the busy, invisible life under the frozen ground. Silhouetted branches wavered in the moonlight, and after whispering a blessing over tree fruits, I ate a chocolate-covered macaroon infused with almond and dense with coconut.

Tu b'Shevat Menu (2018)
Chicken breasts with spicy apricot glaze
Quinoa and rice with diced prunes and caramelized onions
Rainbow chard with apples and toasted pine nuts
Assorted dried fruits and tree nuts
Dried carob pods
Olive-thyme bread
Olives

Fresh fruits: pomegranate, Asian pear, star fruit, apples,
   golden kiwis, blood orange
Poached pears in spices and wine
Coconut-almond macaroons
Maple cookies
Carob brownies
Whole coconut
White and red wines/non-alcoholic sparkling grape, pear,
   and apple juices
Centerpiece: flowers, fruits, nuts, in fruit- and-flower-motif
   bowls; candles

Tu b'Shevat Menu (2023)
Arugula salad with roasted figs, pistachios, goat cheese, and
   maple vinaigrette
Avocado and citrus fruit salad
Wild mushroom and barley soup
Almond-stuffed dates
Carob chip cookies
Chocolate ice cream balls rolled in toasted coconut
Rosé wine
Apple cider
Centerpiece of mandarin oranges and evergreen sprigs

14

Saltines and Honey Cake

I CONTINUE TO BE SURPRISED at the things that matter to my children. A few days before Rosh Hashanah, my then twenty-year-old and I were chatting on the phone. In a wistful but ironic tone, they expressed a wish for "Co-op honey cake" for the holiday. I resisted, saying that there must be excellent honey cake in Brattleboro, Vermont, where they lived, three hundred miles from home. But it was the "Co-op" part that got me; that's the grocery around the corner where we did much of our shopping when my children were growing up.

I rarely eat honey and even less often with McIntosh apples, but that flavor conjures fall holidays in my parents' home. It is nostalgic, yet the memory also adds to the holidays' magic, layered with time and understanding. So, I think I understood Chrys's wish for Co-op honey cake.

My children were not particularly observant during that time. Yet sometimes, a desire for some measure of ritual bubbled up. My son, a six-hours' drive away at college, planned a potluck holiday meal with friends one autumn and called me several times over the weekend to ask for an explanation of "first cut" brisket, and whether ten pounds was too much, and—texting a picture— was the pointy or square end of the meat better? And my younger one was asking for cake. I wanted to feed these inclinations, for the lighthearted tone belied something beneath the surface of the New Year's honey.

In most years, both with the children and after they left, when summer waned and local apples appeared in markets, I began to plan. A group of friends would gather at my house for brisket on Rosh Hashanah eve, and others would stream through for an open-house buffet to break the fast on Yom Kippur. Not only these High Holidays, but the whole cycle of the Jewish holidays marked my year from September through the following August, and festive meals, whether traditional or improvised, added to the meaning. When one is away from home at any stage of life, such gatherings may feel particularly important. But sometimes, circumstances make it hard to observe. A feast day passes without comment, a holiday ritual is empty, and I feel similarly so.

In the late eighties, having left my first marriage and my first serious job in quick succession, I was rudderless and living in a small apartment with little natural light, the occasional crash of broken windows, the regular thump of loud music from an upstairs neighbor, and the squeal of delivery trucks and shouts of workers loading boxes at five in the morning for a small industry in the alley behind my apartment. I had to get away.

Costa Rica beckoned with its pristine Atlantic and Pacific coasts, rain forests, and friendly reputation. Since childhood, I had wanted to make a pilgrimage to witness the sea turtles arriving to nest on the Nicoya Peninsula. There is something transcendent in the image of bales of heavy-shelled females who heave themselves onto the sand; laboriously dig nests; and, for reasons I've never learned, shed tears as they lay leathery eggs that will yield tiny young that skitter their way to the surf, drawn by an ancient force. Only a small percentage of the hatchlings will survive the gauntlet of predatory birds and sea animals.

At the time, transportation in Costa Rica was spotty, consumer and tourist services were rudimentary, and there were

regular earthquakes, but I wanted to wander this relatively un-
spoiled country with its large swaths of protected parks. With
a travel companion, I planned a trip that happened to coincide
with Passover sometime in the middle of the journey. I hoped
that at the end of my more-than-forty days, I could escape the
narrow place I'd gotten myself into, even if I didn't find a biblical
promised land.

I read books on leaf cutter ants, buttress roots, epiphytic plants,
the distinct ecosystems of forest canopies and dry tropical areas,
the history of Costa Rican cowboys in the West, and the hard-to-
predict arrival of the nesting turtles, the arribada. If I was lucky, I
also hoped to glimpse a sloth or the resplendent quetzal.

We arrived in early spring and headed out of San José. Soon,
we were traversing miles of dusty, denuded hills and fields dotted
with occasional villages. It was well before GPS and cellphones:
we kept our Rand McNally map open on the dashboard to become completely confused by unnamed dirt roads that weren't
on the map and distances that didn't quite match the guidebook's
directions. The "paved" road was rutted—not with potholes but
seeming crevasses—so the twists and turns and the sudden rise
of the hills required the driving skills of Evel Knievel and possession of a more rugged vehicle than our cute little rental car with its
shuddery shift and questionable transmission. We quickly learned
to lead the automobile in a jerky dance: front wheel to the edge of
the right-hand pothole, dip a bit to skip the larger chasm on the
left, allemande right and do-si-do the next deep split. In the meantime, a scrape and roar signaled approaching vans and trucks that
whipped around the curves and somehow avoided tumbling into
the holes or stalling out, which we'd done a few times.

This drive was among several challenges we'd face in this otherwise hospitable country, including two mild earthquakes that
highlighted the creative electrical wiring on the east coast and
a stomach bug, probably from a dodgy fish meal, that forced me
to undertake a ten-day fast. But I wasn't there for the amenities.

After the last steep, rutted climb on that dicey road, the dry fields ended abruptly, and we were suddenly, gloriously, at the edge of rain forest. Monteverde had not yet become a major tourist destination, so it was quiet except for birds and insects. My journey had begun.

The next morning, we hiked into the forest, our footsteps muffled by thick beds of enormous leaves and accompanied by the twittering and caw of birds and the glitter of sapphire-blue morpho butterflies in the dappled light. At the edge of a clearing, we glimpsed a bright flash of blue and red high in a tree. I got my binoculars out in time to spot a cluster of resplendent quetzals, flashing their magnificent tails and dipping and weaving in the canopy. At night, insects and frogs formed a chorus like nothing I'd heard, and with no artificial light in the area, the sky was dense with stars.

We had anticipated spending Passover in San José. It was a natural crossroad as we traversed the country, and although I knew a seder would be different from my extended family's elaborate dinner and service, it could be meaningful. We'd obtained the name of a friend of a friend, an American who'd been living in San José for several years, whom we planned to call and ask for suggestions. I was curious to see how people adapted the seder to the locale. The balmy weather and landscape differed from the spring season at home, but this appealed to me, dramatizing the sense of a global community celebrating an ancient ritual, all at the same time. I imagined either finding a small gathering of locals and expats or perhaps being invited to a home seder. It would be a highlight of the trip.

Let all who are hungry come and eat, says the Haggadah, the story and guide for the Passover feast. As a symbol of welcome and hospitality, we open the door once for Elijah the prophet and a second time for *all who are needy come to celebrate Passover with us.* In the Exodus tale, Jews wandered without a home, and a modern take on this suggests we should consider all who are in need, all who are hungry, all who suffer injustice. While we two travelers were certainly not hungry or deprived, we were far from home and looking for a pleasant seder. It is a holiday of inclusion and generosity, and a secular reflection of that is an expanding table of guests.

So, I was dismayed when we called this American couple and were met not with an open door but an indifferent, if polite, dismissal. Yes, we were two twenty-somethings wandering Central America, and she didn't know us. But we were away from family during a time when people usually gathered and were perhaps feeling a little travel fatigue. I had hoped for something like a referral to a community seder, or maybe an invitation to their table. Instead, she gave me the number for a tour group at a hotel that served a Passover meal. She thought it was $60 per person to attend (the equivalent of about $139 in 2023). But we were on a budget. Besides, the thought of listening to someone intone a watered-down version of the seder through a crackling microphone for a bunch of Americans in a hotel sparked my reverse snobbishness—but also wistfulness. These decades later, I am chagrined at my presumptuous self-righteousness. But the yearning was real.

We debated what to do and decided to look for matzah and some equivalent of the other ritual foods to make our own mini seder. But a search for matzah yielded nothing, and we soon got tired of wandering around, going in and out of stores trying to explain what we were looking for.

That evening, we ended up in a nondescript restaurant and ordered a bland chicken soup that came with saltines. I tried to make the best of it, and sotto voce, we sang a few rounds of "Dayenu," the ritual song that translates loosely as "it would have been enough." But the taste of salty, yeasted crackers was not only nowhere near matzah, it contradicted the ritual of avoiding leavened bread. I was depressed. We ate the soup and tried to say a few blessings, but it wasn't enough.

Our trip was only partly over though, so we left the city and, in the following weeks, explored coral reefs dense with fish and anemones; dry tropical landscapes; and forested islands noisy with howler monkeys that perched on stone walls, clutched pieces of fruit, and stared at us. Above a vast active volcano, I watched lava bubble and seethe, sending up splashes of orange plumes and clouds of smoke and ash. I felt I was really on a planet in a way I never had. One can read about such things, but hearing, smelling, and seeing an active volcano is to take in the awe-inspiring reality of Earth, which is changing beneath our feet all the time. In later years in a northeastern forest, I imagined magma deep below the layers of oak and maple leaves, soil, and bedrock.

We encountered more dynamic nature, beyond anything guidebooks could have conveyed; moreover, people we met went beyond the bromide reputation of "friendly" that guidebooks tend to use, no matter the nationality. Although the door to an actual seder had not opened for us, Costa Rican people welcomed us in other ways. At a roadside stand, a woman sold hand-painted pottery made from coils of red clay, and taking in our dusty clothes and large backpacks, she offered us some strong black coffee. I bought a small, terra-cotta pot with a black painted design, its imperfections making it more beautiful.

Another day, somewhere on a hike, a screw came out of my eyeglasses, and one of the temples detached. Myopic and astigmatic, I'm useless without my glasses. I couldn't find the screw anywhere, and my prescription sunglasses wouldn't cut it driving at night on a dirt road or hiking shady forests. At the next town, we naïvely inquired about an optician. A man told us there were none. "In fact," he said in Spanish, "I don't know anywhere you could get glasses, except maybe San José." I realized that I hadn't seen many people wearing glasses. While the government provided universal basic health care, services like glasses and dental work were probably beyond the budget of many Costa Ricans at the time. The man chatted with us, then stopped to think. "No optician," he said, "but we do have a jeweler."

In the tiny shop, a man was working silver on a jeweler's anvil. I showed him my glasses, and he asked us where we were from and what our itinerary was. He smiled. Philadelphia, he exclaimed, the Liberty Bell! He then urged us to visit a small town in the northwest corner of the country. We didn't fully understand what he was saying, something about hundreds of birds and music, but we assured him we'd check it out. He quickly reattached the temple to my glasses, polished the lenses and handed the glasses back with a friendly nod. Despite my pleas to accept more, the jeweler would take only my thanks and a promise to go see "the birds and the music" in the Guanacaste town.

At dusk several days later, in the town he'd recommended, we witnessed thousands of birds flocking to the roofs and telephone wires around the central plaza, competing in sound with clusters of musicians who played a transcendent mix of songs with instrumental accompaniment, including various strings, oboe-like winds, and something with a single-stringed bow and a gourd-resonator. Voices harmonized and echoed across the plaza.

On the Caribbean coast one evening, weeks later, we encountered a group of local and expat wanderers and, late into the night, got into a conversation that one has only in one's twenties, when we're developed enough to think abstractly but not jaded enough to temper wild speculation and naïve leaps of faith. As we debated religion, nature, human folly, and politics, I had one of those elusive moments that slip through your consciousness like a falling star in your peripheral vision—you grasp at it, and some spiritual Heisenberg principle makes it impossible to see the phenomenon directly. It was a glimpse, a liminal moment between the physical world and the transcendent—language is inadequate to the experience. The sense hovered on the crest and dip of the gentle waves, the laughter and music. I had a warm sense of well-being and—admittedly through a haze of cheap beer—a momentary understanding of something people call God. Or something like that. While my persistently logical brain immediately dismissed it, the sensation floated at the edges of consciousness. Then it was gone, leaving only the knowledge that it had been there.

I am, at most, agnostic, and the experience put few dents in my bedrock empiricism but, nevertheless, added complexity to my beliefs. In retrospect, this moment might have been a glimmer of the Divine, but also a symptom of the wretched stomach illness that hit me the next day. But still, the experience was real.

Way past midnight, the little group lay on the sand, plucked guitars, and watched the bowl of stars move slowly above us.

Along with natural wonders, these kinds of encounters gave me the peace I had sought and, like other extended travel I'd taken, refreshed my perspective on life. Nevertheless, though my acute disappointment of Passover faded, it was not erased. Something had been missing, and that stayed with me for a long time. Sometimes, we can make do with saltines, but I missed having Passover. And we ended up missing the arribada, too.

15

Leavening

I WAS PUSHING MY THIRTY-THREE-POUND TODDLER in a rickety stroller up a steep hill at noon on a hot September day in southern Provence. The three-year-old, happy in their transport, hummed a repetitive tune; I sweated and squinted in the glare, a heavy shopping bag slung over one shoulder, and another looped on a wrist. This three-kilometer trek was our daily lunch commute from Chrys's nursery school to our tiny house on the hill. We stopped to rest near the top of the hill, and I took in the expanse of the Mediterranean, the scallop-shaped harbor, bright colored boats bobbing along the docks, terra-cotta roofs, stone church tower against the sea, a cluster of sheep on a hillside. Chrys pointed to an emerald-hued lizard that darted across our path.

The view was spectacular, but besides a swig of water, what kept us going was the crisp baguette I pulled from the shopping bag. Sometimes Chrys wanted the heel, sometimes the second piece torn from the long, warm bread. Baked only hours ago, the crisp crust gave way to a toothsome, light crumb. I never tired of this bread and have never had anything like it since. I learned to ask for *bien cuit* ("well-cooked"), browner than some like but so crisp, it sprayed crumbs when you broke it and gave Chrys something satisfying to gnaw on for the rest of our journey.

By the time we reached the gate to our house, we'd often finished half the loaf; at lunch, we ate much of the second half. The second (and sometimes a third) was for dinner. After the children were asleep, I'd sit on the patio and eat the last remnants of baguette, alternating between bread and a wedge of creamy, local cheese—a splendid version of the cookies-and-milk problem. Under a black, star-speckled sky, with only the night insects and an occasional owl against the silence, there was no better late night snack.

Bakery bread was regularly on the dinner table during my childhood. Although we lived in a small town with a relatively homogeneous population, two bakeries instilled in me the sense that bread was something more than just starchy calories or something spongy to absorb the mayo from a tuna salad sandwich.

On a side street near our quiet downtown was a square brick building with a glass storefront that you'd pass if you didn't know any better. Iuliano's, an Italian bakery that had opened in 1922, sold simple, round fragrant loaves that first taught me what "real" bread is. After a stop at the fish market nearby, my mother and I would enter the warm bakery with its yeasty, floury sweet smell. On the way home in the car, I'd sniff the bread through the white paper bag. Its crisp but slightly chewy crust and a substantial crumb stood up to anything you'd want to load on it. When we asked what was for dinner, my mother might list some main course and sides—I can't recall how that sounded—but I do recall the way she said "Iuliano's" with something like an Italian pronunciation. Never "bread" or "Italian bread." *Iuliano's.*

For my paternal grandfather, bread was the foundation of a meal. If there was none on the table, no matter the meal, he would smile slowly and ask, "So where's the bread?" What he meant was a sliced, very fresh rye bread dotted with caraway seeds, stacked on a small plate and close enough to reach throughout the meal and slather with what must have been margarine in those days. If anyone would be a judge of excellent rye bread, it was my Pop

Hy, one of eight children in an orthodox Jewish family, who lived much of his life on the Lower East Side and in Brooklyn.

The Parkade Bakery in my hometown had such a bread. The name referenced the bland, sixties-era shopping center that belied the magic of this Jewish bakery that opened in 1968 by a family who, coincidentally, lived across the street from my family. Everyone, whatever their background, frequented the store. On Sunday mornings after church, people lined up outside the small shop; the bakery gave out tickets to reserve bread, rolls, bagels, rugelach, and enormous chocolate chip cookies.

Chewy, substantial, with crunchy caraway seeds, a tawny crust, and a faint, pleasant sourness, the rye formed the best sandwiches at my childhood house and was served for some holidays and dinners; there was always at least half a loaf in the freezer. As a child, my favorite way to eat leftover rye bread was for breakfast, well-toasted, browned and crisp, with melting margarine and a thick coat of cinnamon sugar.

On Friday nights, we ate challah from the Parkade Bakery. Like Iuliano's, this challah set the bar for what bread should be. The braided loaf was golden with only a hint of sweetness, dense without being doughy, enrobed in a glossy crust, and large enough for leftover toast on the weekend. Along with the rye bread and Iuliano's, this was real bread.

Those breads are my holy grail, and like the baguette decades later, spoiled me for bakeries. When I bite into a piece of challah, if it's too mushy or without a proper, thin crust or not golden enough or crumbles when you butter it, I continue searching. A rye that squashes too easily or is too pale or lacks the chewy crust, a baguette that doesn't leave crust crumbs on the table when you break it or lacks that je ne sais quoi is not the real thing. But it is more than culinary standards and the pleasure of eating that make bread important.

While many foods from our past elicit memories, bread seems particularly entwined with meaning, given its primal nature and link to ritual. Bread figures in a number of religious practices, from challah at Friday night Shabbat to the "bread" of the Eucharist, which derived from the unleavened bread eaten at the Last Supper (i.e., Passover). The word *bread* is a stand-in for sustenance or food in some religions and cultures. In the English language, we "put bread on the table" or earn "bread" (money), and we "break bread" to commune with strangers and friends.

Like strands of challah dough, memories are braided into the meaning of rituals, and actual bread evokes both meaning and memory. At times, we may seek an elusive ideal from the past—a cardamom-scented coffee cake, a fluffy pita—along with innocence, family, that first kiss, a transcendent moment. In tasting "the" bread, we relive the joys and grief of our past.

So, eating bread in a family or community can provide a glimmer of past moments and of present meanings, but the act of making bread may go a step further to enhance and create ritual experiences.

I've rarely made yeast bread. Perhaps my first, brick-like products discouraged further effort; besides, there always seemed to be a relative or friend—my oldest sister in the seventies, my children's father in the nineties, a friend in the 2010s—who baked and shared their bread. So, my thoughts about the process are from observation and what others have told me.

For decades, my maternal uncle baked weekly bread until, in his eighties, he became too infirm to do so. He was the first person I'd watched up close making a yeast bread. At my parents' house one holiday weekend, probably in the seventies, you could smell the dough being prepared in the kitchen. He'd add some flour or water, other ingredients, knead it, pat two pieces of dough into rounds in large bowls covered with dish towels, and place them in our utility room, which was warmer than our kitchen with its inadequate metal-framed, uninsulated windows. Later that day, I watched him punch down the dough and let it rise again. That night, we ate the bread with its thick crust, hearty crumb, a mix of grains.

My uncle was, at one time, also a fine, amateur woodworker, another endeavor that requires patience, repetition, muscle, and a feel for what works. He was one of the calmest, most patient men I've known, with a soft voice (although when we were children, he would, on demand, make a credible mooing sound like a cow, which cracked us up). I imagined him in his home woodworking studio, sanding and planing a plank of walnut until the grain emerged, carefully mitering it with trim, adding the legs to a graceful table. And with bread, I imagined him creating a new mix of grains, kneading the dough, adding a bit more of this or that until the feel of the dough was correct. Both furniture and bread are useful objects, but those objects and the process of making them are imbued with the individuality, love, and meaning of something handmade, and sometimes, that meaning is intensified by the larger context.

In the first year of the COVID pandemic, friends and family began to bake bread. Apparently, my community was not alone: a flour shortage occurred in the spring, not only from supply-chain problems but also from an overwhelming demand. When I mentioned that I couldn't get any flour at my local grocery, my older sister, who lives in Florida, sent me a pound of "artisanal" organic flour, the only kind she could get. I used it up, though I never did learn to make bread.

I expect that some people baked bread out of necessity during that time, but bread baking is also soothing. It requires muscle, and kneading dough is a repetitive, meditative—for some—activity. The act of baking slows one down because you have to wait for the dough to feel just right and then for it to rise. At every stage, from proofing the yeast to rise to baking, it smells good, and nothing tastes as good as homemade bread. It provides physical nourishment and psychic comfort. Perhaps that's why some also took up brewing or knitting, physical acts that yield an aesthetically pleasing and comforting product.

But after the beer- and ice-cream-making gadgets started to gather dust, after the Peloton machines piled up in warehouses, bread baking persisted.

Why did people continue after the urgency passed? At that time, my middle sister had learned challah baking from her daughter, Rose, and continued making it. She loves the smell, the process of kneading and learning complex braiding techniques and says it is her favorite part of Shabbat. Some of my friends continued baking bread as well. They find it deeply satisfying to create dough from a few simple ingredients, enjoy the sensory and physical act of kneading, and the magic of the rise and the transformation from dough to crumb through baking. It is not a chore but a pleasure they happily anticipate.

But there is something more: baking bread feels meaningful to these cooks in arduous and in good times, and giving away home-baked bread feels different from, say, depositing canned goods at a food bank. Bread making is more than therapeutic, although healing is a close cousin of ritual.

Baking bread has a primal quality to it, with features that constitute a robust ritual: it's an ancient, physical practice involving the senses, nourishment, and repetition. One bakes bread for celebrations, mourning, and other life passages, with family or community, and bread baking may continue a tradition over generations. An informal baking practice marks the day or the week, too. Home-baked bread is delicious, but it's also time-consuming, often unnecessary, and inefficient—as many good rituals are. The act itself matters.

There can be something else, too, that infuses bread with additional layers of meaning. Like other distinctive breads, challah has assumed different forms across cultures and time—from a flatbread in the ancient Levant to the glossy, braided mound many North Americans eat today—and, in some traditions, by necessity or choice, people have used a starter instead of yeast: a fermented piece of reserved dough that aids the rising process by emitting carbon dioxide bubbles. Then, a piece of the new, risen dough is kept for the following weeks.

There is an apocryphal tale, but it is a myth I embrace. Challah starters were said to have been handed down from parent to child over generations, maybe even stowed away on ships leaving Europe for the US. Perhaps even now, a smidgen of the same, ancient molecules our ancestors touched have been handed down over a millennium to be baked into the next generation's challah. What could be more fundamental, providing not only a legacy but also a foundation for ritual that you can hold in your hand?

My brother, Aaron, notes that during the pandemic, he experimented with sourdough starters for rolls and bread: he mixed water and flour, put it on his household water heater, discarded two-thirds of it every few days, and added more flour and water each time until it started bubbling after about ten days. In an email, he wrote, "It was pretty exciting when it finally became 'alive'! I just have to keep feeding it every week or so or it will die." In early 2023, he was still using the same starter at his restaurant in the Pacific Northwest, a business he opened with cautious optimism in the summer of 2020.

While I recognize that making starters may be a creative challenge or a necessity for some, it also may hint at something else: a yearning for living things to bubble and grow, come to fruition, nurture and delight us, a yearning for continuity, even in the midst of difficulties. The act of keeping a starter and baking bread with it—even if partly derived from necessity or boredom—is perhaps an avowal of hope and care.

But back to the Parkade Bakery, the source of the weekly challah in my youth, for there's more to the story. Braided into that story is a tale of bread baking not only as potential delight, therapy, or ritual but also of humanity, love, and survival.

In 1940 in the Warsaw ghetto, food was scarce, and the Gestapo terrorized Jewish people. But one Jewish family continued to run their bakery as well as they could, despite the harassment, the shortages, and the uncertainty of their future. A young man, Yusho, helped his father produce the loaves in that bakery, secretly sustaining the nutrition of their neighbors in the ghetto. Among these neighbors was a young woman, Heluchna, who caught the eye of Yusho and whose mother encouraged the budding romance. At least you will eat, her mother said.

But the couple was soon torn apart, Yusho sent to Bergen-Belsen concentration camp, and Heluchna, to Auschwitz. Emaciated, sick, and destined for the gas chambers, Yusho caught the attention of the commandants because he was a baker. He survived Bergen-Belsen by baking bread for his jailers, his torturers.

Except for one of his brothers, who eventually made his way to the US, Joe and Helen, as they came to call themselves, were the only members of their families to survive the Holocaust.

United in 1945 after the war, Helen and Joe journeyed to Paris and, after a few years, to Connecticut, eventually settling on my street, where they raised two children, one of whom was my friend. And they opened the Parkade Bakery, where perfect challah, chewy rye, and enormous, crisp chocolate chip cookies graced the Shabbat tables and Sunday after-church dinners in our small town. Each bite of bread and cake from their hand was a blessing.

16

Under the Tent

IN MARCH 2020, I was on Cape Cod for my spring break from teaching, with nothing to do but read, walk on the beach, and write. It was quiet off-season, although news had seeped into my awareness: an odd virus had shown up in the Northwest. But I assumed this disease would hold the attention of the press for a few weeks, be contained, and fade from memory.

Over the next five days though, the numbers swelled. My university campus closed abruptly, and the administration announced we would teach online for the rest of the semester, with something called "Zoom."

At home, I oriented myself as well as I could to online teaching, ditched most of the remaining syllabus, and spent an exhausting first week feeling like an untrained airline pilot as I juggled various screens and applications, and more so, tried to manage the anxiety visible in the tiny videos of my students, as they hunched on living room couches, at dorm desks, and in their beds, accompanied by stuffed animals, pets, and younger siblings.

On the weekends, I tried to see my mother at her care facility, where we were eventually permitted to "visit," but only on the phone through a window. In the evenings, I forced myself to catch up on the news and witness the images of refrigerated morgue trucks, the tired eyes of health care workers above their masks, families pressing palms to the windows of dying relatives' hospital rooms.

My sense of isolation was wearing. I missed the serendipitous chats with colleagues, students dropping in at my office, dinners with friends in my neighborhood, casual conversations at the grocery. More and more, I yearned for my regular Friday night services with fellow congregants.

Soon, an email announced online religious services at my synagogue. I was determined to participate, especially since the week happened to coincide with the fourth anniversary of my father's death. I put on a decent shirt, earrings, and lipstick, positioned my laptop on the dining room table with a background of the trees out my window and a small flower arrangement at my side, and tried to log in. But I couldn't get the link, and I panicked, desperate to be there when the service started and desperate to say Kaddish. I tried everything and finally called one of my tech gurus, my son.

He told me to switch computers, and magic—there I was, another tiny box with a face, just as the group began singing Psalm 95.

The rabbi sat at his home, a decorative cloth hung on the wall behind him. It was a larger Friday gathering than usual. Seeing people's faces, even on screen, hearing the familiar melodies and the rabbi's wry humor, I began to cry. I turned off my camera, not wanting to distract others, although I could see that many were moved. During Kaddish, the swell of voices gave me a sense of serenity I hadn't felt for a while.

But in a few weeks, Fridays would arrive, and I had to push myself to log on, and eventually, I stopped attending the services. I was, as they say, Zoomed out, that peculiar oxymoron. We were all going nowhere fast.

In early summer, both of my children were home, and in the evenings, we sat on the back porch and by candlelight, watched the fireflies rise from the ground and listened to soothing pod-casts of short stories, punctuated by the ratchet of helicopters, the crack of fireworks, the screech of speeding cars, and the sirens, as the protests following the killing of George Floyd exploded across the city, and a six o'clock curfew was dumped onto the pandemic lockdown.

By fall, I had learned to limit what I did online and managed my teaching so that I wasn't completely spent by the end of each day. Online, I met with friends for a casual book club, and eight childhood chums reunited for a regular chat. At the High Holidays that fall, I put services on in the background while I cooked for a party of one.

Another whole year rolled by, the autumn holidays returned, and temple leadership decided that High Holiday services would be held in person, outdoors.

The first service in the fall holiday cycle is the penitential *S'lichot*, which my congregation observed as a musical event with an array of international, ancient, and contemporary melodies. That evening, a friend and I walked at sunset to the synagogue grounds. Rising in the night in front of us was a large white tent with three open sides. Interior lights formed a warm glow. The murmur of voices and the tuning of stringed instruments greeted us.

The white tent seemed to draw the smaller-than-usual congregation together as we took our seats in rows of folding chairs and waved across the aisle to friends. It had rained in the afternoon, so most of us were in sneakers or boots; no one was dressed up. Fancy didn't matter. It felt intimate, with everyone clustered underneath.

Perhaps we felt safer in the public health sense, but a tent is more than a practical solution. Tents signal circuses, fairs, wedding receptions. Tents are also fragile but protective, temporary but welcoming, rudimentary but cozy. Sleeping in a tiny tent years ago, my children and I watched a full moon rise over the Negev Desert; in another tent, at another time, in the Pennsylvania woods, we listened to the katydids and frogs.

The tent at that autumn service also felt like a sign of the season, its transient structure reflecting the transient nature of our lives and its existence connoting a strong biblical image—the tabernacle, the tents of my forebears. Vulnerability, protection—and the central theme of this service, asking forgiveness—not only marked the holiday but also seemed deeply thematic of that particular era we were living through.

The leaders stood behind Plexiglas shields, but microphones conveyed their welcoming spirit, their mirth. The people around me were animated, and I was glad to be outside at night.

The oud player began a soft chromatic refrain; the bass picked it up. The oud's slow tremolo was a soothing rain of sound, the song leaders added their quiet harmonies, and the congregation joined in. Our masks muffled the words, but the hum of our voices rose and was amplified by the tent ceiling, and with the drum, we increased the tempo and volume of the chorus. I felt as if the sound spread through my body.

Under the tent, I heard the sweet tenor voice of a person behind me, felt bass notes of song thrum in my chest, and the conga drum reverberated. The pizzicato of the oud and the harmonies of the singers were like a caress. A cool breeze broke the month-long heat wave, and for the first time in eighteen months, I experienced the physical presence of a group of people.

The first song ended, and the rabbi sighed happily into the microphone. "We have really missed this," he said.

Being outside under the tent added a new emotional tone, but the sound itself was also different than indoors and enhanced the service: the tent rendered a faint, pleasant echo and more subtle dynamics; and ambient noise was intensified. The rustle of our song sheets became a gentle percussion to song.

In this sense, what I experienced under the tent was perhaps analogous to LPs versus digital recordings. The first time a friend gave me earbuds to hear digital music, I was astonished. The sound of the piano was crystalline. Yet over time, I sometimes preferred LPs with their richness, their lack of purity, and the sense of the recording as an event preserved in sound, as if you can feel the size of the concert hall or recording studio. Apparently, LPs have that layered, in-person feel because the complete sound wave has been recorded; we are hearing not a close sampling of it, as with digital renderings, but the original wave itself.

For decades, I've owned a record of János Starker playing Bach's Cello Suites. You can hear the bow's action on the strings, sometimes percussive, sometimes a thrumming rasp, then velvety, and the occasional shush of his fingers sliding down the strings. At several points, he sighs, an audible note. One also hears a sigh on the LP recording of the "Koln Concerts" by the pianist Keith Jarrett.

And under the tent, the rabbi sighed.

When I listen to the Bach record, it is this human aspect—not just the music itself—that washes over me and imparts relaxation, satisfaction, and meaning. Under the tent at the religious service, I experienced the full sense that comes with being "in person"—a phrase more resonant than its mere technical connotation.

Under the tent, I heard the full sound wave but, moreover, felt a nonempirical, elusive thing that perhaps arrives not only with the combination of the five senses but also with the experience of being physically in community. In the immediacy of collective prayer and song, something swelled and rose as we progressed through the service. Under the tent, I felt a wordless, collective optimism and poignant joy—perhaps, for some, a sacred presence.

The final note of the service lingered in the air and faded, and we could hear the night insects chirping. The group seemed to sigh as one. Seeing the soft reflection of lights on the white ceiling of the tent, I anticipated the holiday that comes late in the Season of Awe: Sukkot (Feast of Tabernacles), a week of eating, singing, and praying in an outdoor, fragile booth, at home.

Ufros aleinu, sukkat shlomechah, says the prayer. *Over us, oh God, spread your shelter of peace.*

17

White Coat, Black Book

I WONDER IF MY CLASSMATES from graduate school remember their first psychotherapy clients. Given the number of decades since, I am surprised that I recall the college student who spoke in a whisper and kept their coat on during the whole hour with me, despite the overheated, windowless room where we met. Maybe because my anxiety came close to matching theirs, as I sweated and repeated a silent mantra to myself ("Don't mess up!"), the memory of that early session was indelible. After two years of research and classroom theory, lectures on the clinical interview, and a lot of practice doing psychological evaluations on each other, we trainees were plopped into the on-campus mental health clinic as staff. My client and I survived.

My classmates and I were not without close supervision, nor do I think we were completely unprepared. My clinical professor on that early case was a practical, clean-shaven man with starched dress shirts, an academic interest in nontraditional healing and psychoanalysis, and the occasional appearance of dry humor. He critiqued my therapy session sentence by sentence, silence by silence. But something was missing from my experience, something to mark what was, for me, a momentous shift, the beginning of duty to someone's heartache, relationships, desires. As I trained to be a therapist, I witnessed people in what they thought were their worst moments (or their best), and heard stories they'd perhaps told no one else.

No ritual defined my passage into this professional life, no indication that I might be transformed by the work. A parent, a child, a couple, a teen would trust me with their fears, their intimate stories, their shame, and their joy. And they would trust, too, that I might help them. I wished in those early months that there was some ritual for beginning this sacred task, perhaps at the beginning of my clinical placements or even the start of school when it was just classroom learning. Receiving my diploma some years later didn't cut it; that was about the academy, not the clinic.

By contrast, my niece and nephew began medical school with notable ceremony. Recently, I was weeding through photographs and found two pictures of Rose and Abraham, taken in 2016 and 2018, respectively. Rose is surrounded by friends, and Abraham is flanked by his parents. They are each sporting a short, boxy, white jacket and a wide smile.

Like many of their contemporaries, they were participating in the "White Coat Ceremony" that inaugurates training at many medical schools. The ceremony was conceived in the 1990s and popularized in the following decades. Before peers, faculty, and family, students recite a modern version of the Hippocratic oath or other affirmations like the Geneva Declaration; in some schools, like my niece's, the incoming class writes its own oath. Although students begin seeing patients only in the third year, part of the ceremony's purpose is to convey that care for patients begins, in a sense, in this first year, so a central rite of passage is to don the short white jacket they'll wear in clinical rotations during the second half of school. When they earn their MD, they are entitled to the knee-length version.

I confess some old envy of medical students who launched their professions with a ritual, but I have questions about the dashing white coat.

Doctors didn't wear white until the late 1800s: black was the standard attire. Like clergy at the pulpit (or the sickbed), physicians in black conveyed the gravitas of a medical encounter, perhaps signaling the meeting's true nature: since medicine had little to offer, a visit with the doctor often portended death rather than healing.

Along with the oaths and speeches, the mass of bright white cotton at the contemporary ceremony reflects the novitiate doctor's responsibility to patient and to society. In that sense, gravitas endures, despite the change in couture—and patients' survival rates.

The switch to white near the turn of the twentieth century coincided with the advent of hygiene practices in medicine, a pragmatic choice (one could bleach a white jacket) but perhaps a metaphor for a modern, "clean," science-based practice. No longer would a blood-and-guts smeared black coat mark the experienced physician who was—despite access to some effective treatments—more like a benediction-bestowing priest than a scientist-practitioner. Innovations like antibiotics probably sealed the deal with white later in the twentieth century. Cutting-edge practice entailed a pristine look, and—no coincidence—white symbolizes purity. The starched white coat may have signaled to patients that their doctors' actions were scientific and dispassionate.

In contemporary medicine, donning the white coat means a student will soon enter the vestibule to the rarified club of physicians: clinical rotations. But to me, these rites are also steps toward ordination into a secular priesthood; the switch from black to white in the last century did not mean completely abandoning a role akin to a person-of-the-cloth or a shaman.

For one, modern physicians can seem to practice divination and produce wonders. They can see and interpret every layer of the physical body, alter genes, dispense chemical potions to rid us of plagues, and perform the awesome task of opening viscera and replacing organs. Even medical jargon, credentials on the wall, and touching a patient's hand may matter: according to social scientists, these seemingly incidental, somewhat symbolic aspects of medicine can influence outcomes like patients' adherence to treatment, recuperation from surgery, and especially, improvement in psychiatric illness, just as blessings and chants, ceremonial objects, and attire are inherent to religious ritual. So, the white coat itself holds potential power.

To extend the religious parallel, doctors are not just serving as secular clergy but also making god-like decisions, at times, deciding who shall live or die (though with ethics boards, patients, and families peering over their shoulders). Working at a children's hospital some years ago, I recall a middle-of-the-night, anguished huddle with the medical team and family to discern if a teenager should receive a risky, experimental treatment or face a high probability of death without it. In that conference room, despite the doctors' palpable sorrow, the white coats may have radiated a holy vibe.

Nevertheless, no medical student signs up to play God: no person should have to make hasty decisions about whom to turn away at overcrowded emergency departments without time for measured discernment.

The white coat's quasi-religious connotation hovers like a ghost in the hospital halls, but its embodiment of sterile objectivity was reincarnated in "evidence-based practice," with all treatments needing empirical justification. At the same time, contemporary education aspires to teach a humane approach including respectful relationships with patients, social and political influences on health, and even the humanities, like literature and theatre.

As a writer and psychologist in medical and premedical education, I was sometimes the fish out of water, although I preferred to think of myself as an amphibian. My place in the ecosystem, though, gave me a chance to witness students' (and a few colleagues') stories, some, heavy with yearning for emotional connection, for a break from the expectation of superhuman endurance, and sometimes a desire to breach a rigid hierarchy. Yes, "someone needs to be in charge," as an attending physician once scolded me. But shouldn't humanity, with all its connotations, be at the head of the team?

Soon after budding physicians don the white coat and begin work on the floors, they may get the message: don't get too involved; care *for* patients, but don't care too much *about* them. Although learning to manage one's emotions is part of professionalism in any job, distancing oneself from a patient and from one's own emotions can go too far.

Whether acknowledged or not, emotion and individual identity are present in the medical encounter, the impersonal white coat notwithstanding; they are harmful in medical care only if avoided. The late essayist Anatole Broyard noted that he wanted to be "a good story" to his doctor. Perhaps this is what patients seek in the medical encounter: for their stories to be heard, for their individuality to be seen. We want to be more than "the knee in bed two," as I overheard myself described when hospitalized for surgery. To receive not just a pharmaceutical communion wafer from a white-garbed high priest of modern medicine but also "communion" in the other sense of the word. When my friend says she "loves" her neurologist, she isn't just talking about diagnostic acumen but also compassion and empathy.

While a myopic view is hazardous to patient health, doctors who ignore their own emotional states are also at risk: chronic stress, substance abuse, and other mental health problems plague medical workers. Despite reforms like decreasing the overwhelming hours and providing some formal, emotional support, students' emerging identities include the message to "just do it." Just do it, regardless of their own health or mental state. But as they are grilled on the science, they may be emotionally fried. While I have felicitous memories of teaching and clinical work, among the challenging moments I recall were meetings with individual students who, with some chagrin, approached me looking shell-shocked or in tears.

A white coat may be easy to clean after an impossible string of nights on the intensive care unit, the death of an infant, or the realization that one has made a mistake, but the moral injury is not so easily remedied. Guarding against both callousness and burnout is a balancing act.

If the white coat is potentially a symbol of intemperate objectivity, perilous avoidance of emotions, elevated status that distances practitioner from patient, and inhuman standards for a doctor in training, should the spiffy jacket follow its somber precursor into the rubbish bin? Some physicians have ditched the white coat, along with antiquated social practices like standing while talking to a patient who is seated. But perhaps this symbol, which reflects and confers realities in the medical world, can be changed.

The white coat does have a crisp collar, handy pockets, and an easily identifiable glow at a distance. Uniforms have their place. But maybe there is another reason not to be so quick to trash the white coat. Despite its potentially insidious meaning, the coat could take on an alternative, salutary symbolism, which discards threadbare connotations. If so, medical students might receive this mantle with full, genuine honor.

On Yom Kippur, Jews often recite a prayer stating that God decides at that moment "who shall live and who shall die" in the coming year. It is the most solemn point in the High Holidays. There is an additional custom that might suggest a new interpretation of the doctor's white coat.

Some Jews wear white during the High Holidays. Traditionally, the white clothing is a simple white robe, called a kittel. It looks like a baggy version of the doctor's white coat but without pockets. In fact, it is a shroud, the very one you will be buried in. Wearing the kittel is meant to evoke humility, contrition, and a reminder of one's mortality, to aspire to better behavior towards others in the new year.

Of course, Judaism is not the only religion or culture to employ white as a sign of mortality or purity. Boatloads of paper have been sacrificed to the analysis of why Herman Melville's whale is white and why humans are sometimes clothed in white at burial and other momentous times.

Could the medical student's white coat come to mean, in part, something like the kittel? While the black coat in former times hinted at the *patient's* mortality, the white one could embody the *doctor's* as well, like the memento mori of the Renaissance. Despite the magic of contemporary medicine, despite the audacity necessary to make decisions about someone else's life and body, doctors are only human, only mortal. And maybe they—and we patients—need to be reminded of it. When the beginning medical students place their arms in the sleeves of the white coat for the first time with a secular "congregation" present, this practice might ritualize not only emerging professionalism but also a commitment to humility and to the full humanity of patients, coworkers, and one's self.

I'd like to add something else to the white coat ceremony, something that revives the color black, though it could also be purple, chartreuse, gold, or rainbow.

Several years ago, in a course on meaning and medicine, my students and I studied poems, fiction, essays, and films to explore the big questions: love, death, work, illness, religion, and humor. The students wrote and shared their own stories and poems, sometimes spontaneously describing the strains of school and training. Even at this early stage, they also described a creeping sense that meaning in their work and in life were eroding.

The final class was at my house with a home-cooked meal. At the end, I gave them each a parting gift, a gel pen and a small, lined notebook with a soft, black cover. With some irony, I introduced a "Black Book Ceremony," and they were invited to use the notebook in the future to jot their thoughts, feelings, poems, stories, and sketches. And I added not an oath but a blessing:

"May you sustain confidence without arrogance, compassion without exhaustion, irony without cynicism, humor without disdain, meaning and heart without loss of scientific rigor. May you keep writing and drawing. May relationships, joy, and satisfaction in work endure. And in moments of doubt, may you look to each other, to community, and to a sense of meaning in whatever form that takes."

After reading those words, I knew my hopes for my young guests were born of my own experience. As for the students, they took in my experimental ritual with tolerant humor, but they were especially pleased to take home leftover chili and cornbread.

18

In the Weeds

ONE SATURDAY MORNING IN EARLY APRIL, aimless and frustrated, I started hacking away at a corner of my weedy garden. Layers of leaves and twigs, tangled ivy, and thorny brambles had taken over. Since I resented a lot that spring of 2020, I figured I'd take it out on the hard earth.

I smashed a hoe into the dry ground, furiously dug at the debris and yanked fistfuls of weeds until I had a crooked rectangle, about ten by fifteen feet. I turned over the dirt and leaned on a shovel, panting and wiping sweat from my forehead. Dirt streaked my arms and face, my shirt stuck to my back, and I had blisters on my palms. But for once in that sorry year, I felt powerful. Here was a little corner of the world that I could—maybe—control.

The next week, I planted butterfly weed, butterfly bushes, milkweed, and other pollinator plants. I lugged large rocks from another neglected corner of the garden and made a semicircle around the edge of what I was optimistically calling my "butterfly garden" to distinguish it from the rest of the unkempt yard. The plants looked bedraggled, drooping in the hot sun and beginning immediately to succumb to the hardy weeds that populated my yard. But maybe later in the summer, I'd get monarchs, swallowtails, and skippers.

I am not a gardener. I occasionally get enthusiastic and work for a little while on my yard, but ultimately, I get bored and just plain lazy. When I walk through my yard and see the weeds and pest-ridden, untended plants, I feel like lying on a couch and watching Netflix. The sight of the particularly recalcitrant bishop's weed makes me anxious.

But there I was, hacking away at the soil in an effort to quell my anger and fear, determined to do something, anything, that wasn't staring at a screen or fretting and being pissed off at the general state of the world. I was even cynical about gardening, but I tried.

By summer, I was surprised to see that my little butterfly garden had survived and grown. Somehow, it had defied the political and public health maelstroms and my lackadaisical care. Of course, by the time I noticed that it was growing, it had become populated by weeds. My fault. I hadn't really tended it properly. Instead of regularly weeding and watering, I'd go out early in the morning just to look, glad to see buds forming on the new plants. I'd notice little green sprouts of weeds and return to my kitchen for a second cup of tea.

Neglect was the wrong word for my approach. Active avoidance was more like it. Every day seemed too hot, my teaching and writing, even housework, too pressing. Inertia, but also a downward spiral. Unkempt gardens bring out all of my feelings of inadequacy.

But one day, the heat broke, and I tried to trick myself into tending the garden. I chose a small bucket and told myself I only had to fill this one container with weeds, once.

I kneeled and began yanking out the culprits. Some of the weeds' runners and roots were so deep and extensive that I strained my shoulders in the process. The bishop's weed had runners that broke off in my hand, and the thorns of other invasive plants pierced my gloves. I looked at the alleged butterfly garden and started to feel that creeping garden fatigue. Nope, I told myself, you just have to do this one bucket.

I filled and emptied the bucket, returned to the garden and reframed the problem. The bucket metric was not going to work because the weeds filled it too slowly, and I was impatient. Instead of a bucketful, maybe I'd just do one or two square feet of weeding. Just one little square. And then have lunch, even if it wasn't lunchtime.

I drew a faint square in the dusty soil. And a phrase popped into my head: this is my *helek*, my little portion in the world, and I don't need to do more than that right now. Just this one or two square feet.

I stood up, stretched, and with that thought, felt calmer.

The Jewish mystics wrote about *ha-olam habah*, the world to come, sometimes thought of as a heaven or at least where souls end up after death. The crucial point here is that, traditionally, all are said to have a "portion" or "share" (helek) in that world to come, and, in this life, we must cultivate our share to prepare ourselves. I don't buy into the idea of a world to come, but what's always intrigued me is this word *helek*, which not only refers to a metaphoric portion or share but also an actual "plot," as in a portion of land. I couldn't avoid the connotation: cultivate your plot now to eventually yield fruits in the place where there will be no toil, no business, no pain, no suffering.

The sages' commentary on working one's helek in this world for the world to come includes the idea that we can cultivate our share in different ways: some study, others take care of the community and those in need, some lead, some plant or make things, others nurture or teach children. Over the years, I concluded that maybe I should tend to what is most meaningful or helpful—that is, my individual passion or gift, if you will, the things I could best contribute.

Although the original idea was that humans were preparing themselves for the next world by doing good deeds in this one, modern commentaries and philosophies interpret this as creating, or at least working toward, a better world in *this* physical world. This contemporary take on the world to come charges us to create actual justice and peace, here and now.

These ideas flitted through my mind, and the butterflies were beginning to flit as well. So, I finished my little portion of the garden—my tiny heaven on earth—washed up, and made an early lunch.

To be truthful, my spiritual epiphany was not accompanied by a horticultural one. I wasn't suddenly bitten by the garden bug and didn't, with a swelling chorus of movie music, spend my days cheerfully and diligently working until my garden rivaled Martha Stewart's pristine landscaping. But I did work at it somewhat that summer, and by fall, it looked a little less like the Addams Family's backyard. And the butterflies, bees, and goldfinches visited. That was enough, because what I liked doing more than working in the garden was squatting down and peering closely to see the proboscis of a butterfly drawing out nectar, various moths skimming over tiny purple flowers, a swallowtail butterfly landing on a cone flower, and bees flitting from bloom to bloom, their legs chubby with gold pollen.

One morning, I discovered something that changed it all: a few tiny caterpillars were climbing the stalks and munching away at leaves on one of the plants. I checked every source I could to make sure: yes, they were monarch caterpillars, enjoying the only plant that serves their whole lifecycle: *Asclepias syriaca*, the common milkweed, with its creamy sap and clusters of mauve blossoms. It did not escape me that the root of the Latin name, *Asclepias*, derives from the Greek god of medicine, Asklepios.

Motivation kicked in. I weeded all around the milkweed, checked three times a day, watered regularly, made sure there were all the other things the caterpillars might need as they grew. And they did grow. They grew rapidly. I wished hard that they'd spin their chrysalides on the milkweed in my garden and I'd get to see the butterflies emerge. I was awed and hopeful.

The milkweed became my private version of Eric Carle's children's book, *The Very Hungry Caterpillar*, and I loved seeing "my" hungry caterpillars munch away, systematically carving tiny half-moons along the edges of the leaves, denuding the plants as they should. After researching what else they'd eat, I brought extra food from other parts of the garden. Their appetite was prodigious, and they grew plump and large. I added small piles of sturdy twigs and flat rocks at angles near the plants in case the caterpillars wanted to pupate nearby.

One morning I went out and near the milkweed, a catbird was pecking around in the dirt. I approached and tried to shoo it away. It turned its head slightly to look at me and merely hopped onto one of the flat rocks that I'd placed in the garden. I glared at the bird and knelt to look at the caterpillars on the milkweed, and there, on the ground, were several almost full-grown caterpillars, their sides punctured, mouths and rears leaking. One was moving a little. I gently scooped it up with a small twig, and it curled around the twig. I placed it on a milkweed leaf, but it soon curled up again and fell to the ground. It stopped moving.

The bird had apparently jabbed the caterpillars with its beak, just enough to mortally harm them, a slow death.

I was furious. The arrogance of this violent catbird who hadn't even eaten any caterpillars but just wounded them and with raised beak and smarmy caw, stood on the flat stone I'd put for the caterpillars. It felt cruel, and all the cruelty of the world was concentrated in those beady eyes that seemed to look at me defiantly.

I clapped and yelled at the catbird until it leisurely flapped away.

Somehow, if the little creatures had disappeared altogether, I'd have felt better: everything needs to eat, even catbirds. But this act felt gratuitous. It had just pecked and left them to die.

I know. I was anthropomorphizing, projecting. Monarchs are poisonous to most birds; the catbird likely took one peck at the caterpillar, and the monarch's protective poison deterred the bird from consuming the whole thing. I don't usually personify nature. But still. Stupid, stupid bird! It didn't even recognize that this wasn't a food source? Squawky, mean bird.

I'd had visions of luminescent, emerald green pupae hanging from twigs and rocks in my garden, and in a few weeks, I'd get to watch the butterflies slowly emerge, dry and unfold their orange, stained-glass-window wings, and fly away to Mexico.

But it wasn't to be. The rest of the caterpillars disappeared, too.

I could not stop thinking about them, those little creatures that hadn't even had a chance to turn into butterflies. It was the children's story darkened by a shadow.

After a while, I put away my garden tools and gloves and thought again about the idea of a portion, my plot in the world, for part of tending one's plot is not just weeding but also protecting the vulnerable. I ordinarily do not moralize the natural world, but for the moment, the catbird stood for badness.

We must tend the portion we can, portions filled with choking weeds and swooping predators, and maybe, just maybe, in this world, not some world to come, we can coax some beauty, something that grows and matures, out of the indifferent soil.

19

Graduation in a Year of Wonders

WHEN SCHOOLS CLOSED IN MARCH 2020, my younger one, a senior in high school who was itching to leave home, sprawled on their stomach on the rug in what we still called "the playroom" and tried to pay attention to online classes. I could hear biology and English teachers cheerleading to engage all the sprawled seniors, who would rather have had the chance to contract *senioritis* instead of staying home to avoid a real disease.

Not only were online classes a drag, but prom, a candlelight dinner, a "senior recognition" ceremony, and other festivities were canceled. Ordinarily in the last month of school at the high school, seniors enjoyed independent, off-site projects instead of regular classes. Chrys had been excited to arrange a volunteer gig at a circus arts program for children in Camden, New Jersey; instead, the class had to write some pointless paper. Skipping school and going to the beach; hanging out with friends late at night; and, most of all, being away from parents: none of those normal spring rites happened. Weekends, the two of us were at home, too much in each other's business. For my eighteen-year-old, it was a spring of one sorry disappointment after another.

The last year of high school is, for many, a time to mark "the last"—exam, bio lab, gym class, paper, lunch hour. A time to anticipate hearing from colleges or job prospects and, in my child's case, circus training programs; a time of anticipation and excitement, where the only letdown would not be getting into one's favorite academic program or not getting the job one wanted. But that year, the uncertainty of whether there would even be college or employment in the fall hung over everything. And graduation day? Uncertain.

When you ask students what they most look forward to about graduation, it's walking across a stage to receive their diplomas. At that moment, they are proudly alone, striding in the spotlight to get parchment in hand. There is a fist pump, a bow, a grin, a cheer from family in the back of a field or auditorium; friends call out a nickname in that inimitably affectionate, inside-joke tone. It is the beginning of autonomy, the inkling of adulthood. It's also a time to party. It seemed none of this would happen.

Eventually, the high school administration announced a "Commencement in Cars," which sounded like a strained aspiration to levity. We were not amused.

Families would be allotted one car each, drive onto the grass at the school, and park within separated slots, indicated with spray-painted lines on the lawn. Families would not be permitted to get out of the cars. Students would stay in the cars until ushered, a few at a time, "socially distanced," to wait along the driveway. They would then walk across the outdoor stage, pause for an official photo, and pick up the diploma at a table where the administration would congratulate each masked student.

Although Chrys would get to cross the stage, it seemed like a drive-in without the movie, a rally without the pep.

I was sad mostly because Chrys was robbed of a rite of passage, but my disappointment also included a private sadness. I wouldn't be able to enjoy trying to find my child in a sea of mortar boards and robes. Like many, I had, for years, imagined a proper graduation, anticipated feeling pride in my child and joy at seeing them proud of themselves; I wanted to experience that tangible click of time in its circle, from childhood and teenage years to the beginning of goodbye, to feel the swelling of the heart that happens in those significant moments. How could I experience that sitting in the back seat of a dusty Volvo station wagon that still smelled vaguely of my former mother-in-law's dog?

But I put on my happy parent face and dutifully sent our extended family the Zoom link for the graduation.

We humans adapt, and we parents can, sometimes, defiantly rise to any challenge to our party plans. I wouldn't let a spiky virus win. Nor, it turns out, would other parents.

A few weeks before Chrys's graduation, an email with the subject line "Top Secret!" arrived from a parent of a junior student at Chrys's school, requesting information about their schedule. Tears came easily that spring, so I reached for another tissue when I read the note and made plans with the parent.

One early morning, we coaxed Chrys out of bed to be dressed and waiting on the front lawn. They hadn't a clue what would happen when, suddenly, two cars, emblazoned with signs, balloons, and school insignia, drove up blaring party music. Parents and teachers got out, shouted good wishes, and raised posters, congratulating Chrys. Strangers who passed beeped their horns when they saw what was going on, whooped greetings out their windows. As Chrys accepted a bouquet of flowers, balloons, and a goodie bag filled with treats and school swag, they were smiling in a way they rarely had that spring. It was an exquisite joy, the kind of joy one feels when a child is celebrated, when a community comes together, when we appreciate an act that is both frivolous and generous (the parents had organized to visit every senior's home).

By the time a package arrived in the mail with more goodies from the school for our senior, I was determined to make graduation day as festive as possible, despite my misgivings about the Commencement in Cars. We'd find alternatives; we'd be extravagant.

Early morning on graduation day, a clear sky and slight breeze augured well: Chrys's new light blue suede oxfords wouldn't be ruined in rain-sodden grass at the ceremony; we'd be able to have our luncheon outdoors on the front porch. My private sorrows about the car graduation had dissipated.

We'd inflated and tied fifty balloons all over the yard before Chrys woke up. What's more festive than the hiss of a helium canister and the swelling of balloons in primary colors? They swayed in a light breeze above shrubs, porch furniture, and railings. Behind the rhododendrons, a yellow balloon bumped against the gray stone of the house, red balloons adorned a lawn chair, and the trees seemed to have sprouted otherworldly flower buds. Against the green of the yard, the balloons resembled a Cristo installation designed by Dr. Seuss.

And when Chrys emerged from the house, it was more than okay. They'd donned their navy-blue high school graduation robe, white hood, and mortar board with tassel, brand-new dress shoes peeking out from under the robes. With a sardonic grin, they accepted their brother's orienting of the mortar board properly. And when they looked around the balloon-decorated yard, their smile was an unselfconscious one that said, yes, I'm a knowing almost-adult but I still delight in magic.

They matter, these traditions. The medieval, Harry Potter–like robes, "Pomp and Circumstance." We mark time and occasion through unique rites and objects. The rarity of their use and perhaps the archaic quality adds to the meaning. They may be rooted in a complicated tradition, but on that day, one's engagement with these rituals says we have achieved something important and are entering a new community, a new phase of life.

And perhaps during that year, that annus mirabilis, that year of wonders, we especially needed those significant, rarely used markers. Singularity as normalcy, as continuity.

At the school, we parked in the preassigned spot on the lawn. Rows of cars around us were festooned with congratulatory banners, balloons, crepe paper. Students leaned out of windows, called to each other; festive music boomed from loudspeakers. A parade of decorated cars, accompanied by processional music— also organized by the junior students and their parents—slowly circled our cars. When the ceremony began, it was real; it was moving. The speeches were more substantive than at most graduations. All the speakers seemed to have taken particular care not to plod tired rhetorical paths. The keynote speaker, Jenna Arnold, deftly wove a genuine message that referred to the pandemic, social justice, and politics but without pablum or vapid exhortation.

And when names were called, students walked individually across the stage. They bowed, beamed, waved to family, thanked Nana, did a little dance, gave a thumbs up, shouted "go 'Roos" (yes, the school's mascot is a kangaroo). Even the international students who had to return home were projected on a large screen when their names were called, and across the globe, many in regalia, hugged their parents. Horns honked, families cheered through open car windows.

The salient image of that day is Chrys, after having received the diploma, wriggling their head and torso out the front passenger window and, face to the wind, chin proudly lifted, looking over the rows of cars with a carefree, blissful expression.

At lunch at home afterward, we shared falafel with every possible garnish from one of Chrys's favorite restaurants, accompanied by a wine punch with lavender simple syrup that I'd concocted. We sat amid drifts of colorful confetti that we'd showered on Chrys when they arrived home from the graduation. They opened gifts with the usual hilarity and sarcasm shared with their brother, and passersby stopped to delight in the balloons and our celebration.

Having celebrated Chrys, it was time to give my niece Rose some semblance of the real thing, too. She had also missed a proper ending to her education. Instead of completing her final placement (rotation) at medical school, enjoying dinners or weekends away with friends, attending graduation on-site, or even having a chance to say a proper goodbye, Rose and her friends had been unceremoniously sent home. Worse, soon after she arrived, her mother, my sister Laurie, was hospitalized with a serious case of COVID, so Rose stayed with her father, eventually tending to her mother through isolation and recuperation at home. Graduation was not a concern right then.

Eventually, the school announced an online commencement. By that time, my sister had recovered, and my niece was living near me, so I invited her to my house to watch the ceremony. We sat on the porch and viewed the somewhat anemic affair, made bearable by Rose's family talking and joking on a parallel call and friends posting messages in the chat. The snarky and the heartfelt comments provided a diversion, but in the end, the conferring of degrees on screen seemed an afterthought. We cheered and waved to each other from our little video rectangles.

Afterward, Rose said, "I just wanted to hear my name called in person and walk across the stage and receive my doctoral hood and diploma, hug my friends, have my parents in the audience. I just wanted to walk across the stage."

So, Chrys and I got to work. We sent a formal Evite to Rose for her "real" graduation, and I poured through YouTube videos to distill the quintessential graduation ceremony.

When Rose arrived that afternoon in June, she wore a flowered dress and shiny shoes; I had also emerged from my Zoom cocoon of sweatpants and scruffy slippers to don real pants and shoes. On the front wall of my house, I had fixed a rudimentary sign with her school's name, along with a fictitious branch of her institution—the "Mt. Airy Campus" (my neighborhood). My graphic design skills are as excellent as they were in first grade and commensurate with kindergarten-level technical skills, but I'd managed to embed the school emblem and, using an old set of my children's felt-tip marking pens, hand-colored the insignia in the school colors. Rose happily took a selfie next to the sign.

Chrys served as tech support and followed my written stage directions, such as, "Phone video: welcome logo and voice-over . . . Computer link: start processional music." The two of us had rehearsed once that morning.

Rose wore an old mortar board, maybe from high school, and I lent her Chrys's high school robes, the blue of which was close to one of Rose's school's colors. I'd also repurposed Chrys's white hood from the high school graduation just a few weeks prior and glued on colored fabric trim that was probably from one of my children's old Halloween costumes for a proper doctoral hood.

I instructed Rose to wait next to the pink azaleas below the porch, and at my signal, she walked towards the steps to a You-Tube recording of "Pomp and Circumstance." My inadequate computer speaker rendered the tune faint and tinny but recognizable. Chrys led the processional, and I walked backward, filming a shaky phone video. The candidate perched on the porch in her designated seat decorated with crepe paper in school colors in front of my lawn chair "podium."

I began, "As president, provost, chancellor, vice-president, dean, faculty, distinguished guest, and director of campus IT . . ." Then I welcomed the graduate, provided a brief encomium to her, and even briefer advice. She laughed, teared up, and smiled indulgently at all the right moments. Chrys filmed everything to share with family.

The graduate was then invited to rise when her name was called; I called her name, vested my powers, and conferred her degree. She flipped the tassel to the other side, marched the ten feet across the porch to a table with her actual diploma, which had arrived that week; donned her homemade hood; and, grinning, with diploma in hand, turned for photos. Finally, I introduced a "special guest," and Chrys fired up Beyoncé belting out "I Was Here."

Rose told me it was better than any campus graduation could have been.

Sometimes, we make the effort and do it anyway. We defy incursions on our joy. The attire, the incantations, and perhaps most of all, the act of trying to create these moments, however rudimentary, renders meaning. Perhaps then we can sense the shift from the before times to now, from being a student to becoming a real doctor or a real high school alum.

It's not necessarily a good thing that by the time my son's college graduation came a year later, in 2021, I had gotten used to online meetings. Yet hearing that we families would receive not tickets and actual seats but, instead, a YouTube link for the commencement, I was dismayed.

I wanted to be there, hear his name echo across the lawn, see him with his friends, hug him right away, take pictures, witness his elation, feel proud of him in the moment. I wanted to rush around shepherding the family to catch a fancy lunch. Even Chrys's Commencement in Cars now seemed preferable. *In person*, I demanded of the ether, *not* "remote"—a nasty word. These things were meant to be done in large groups, not sitting alone watching TV in one's living room. "It matters," I yelled at the universe. But the gods were not listening, and I knew that my refusal to accept the inevitable was as much a flailing protest at the world's cruelties—for there were many people far worse off than I—as it was disappointment in graduation plans.

Though I resisted, it dawned on me that at college graduations, parents should be in the background anyway, and while it's wonderful to be there to witness the ceremony, it was, in fact, about Noah and his peers, not me. Young adults are mature enough to express appreciation to their families, and perhaps they sort of like having us there, but they're also itching to celebrate and share a meaningful goodbye with their friends on their own, without us hovering and beaming and snapping pictures.

When the day arrived, I was grateful for the college's prudence in insulating the graduates—and the city's residents—from hordes of out-of-towners. That June morning, I logged on and watched a colorfully dressed, exuberant marching band lead the candidates down a main street. While the president and provost were alone on the dais to greet the candidates, viewers could watch individual students approach, and there were close-ups of them receiving diplomas. When my son's name was called, I had to wipe away tears to see his indelible smile. The school had also arranged to show what graduates were up to behind the podium after they crossed the stage: congratulating each other, throwing their caps in the air, hugging. When the focus was on the podium, we could still hear them cheering and whooping, and the president's delight was evident as she waited for the noise to subside to call the next candidate. Periodically, the cameras would cut away to the band, who provided a boisterous interlude.

No, I didn't get to stand with Noah in his cap and gown for photos or sit among a bustling audience on a New England campus. But I have a screenshot of my son on stage, turning to the cameras for a photo. Blurry as it is, I can see his pride and exhilaration in the moment. At that moment of crossing the stage, his classmates knew their worth, their power (in the best sense of the word), and their possibilities.

And several weeks later, we met at my son's apartment in Providence to celebrate all the happy events of the previous fifteen months. It was my first time seeing both children together in half a year. Vaccinations had arrived; we could hug each other. It was enough that we were alive and safe. It was enough that the children had passed into their next phase of life. It was a time of wonder.

20

Kappa and Saint Anne

I HAVE A FIGURINE ON MY DESK that stares at me while I work. It's less than three inches tall, sculpted clay with matte green, brown, and white glaze. It's almost seventy-five years old. Kappa is a mythical creature with scrawny, reptilian arms scrunched akimbo in a posture as aggressive as his scowl. He leans back on his carapace and guards a fried egg on the ground in front of him. Should you venture near his breakfast, so the story goes, he will snatch you, particularly if you are a child, and pull you down into his swamp to drown.

This diminutive, nasty creature observes every typed word, every glance out the window, every page I open in a book. At times, I have imagined him saying, "Ha, you call yourself a writer? Your sentences aren't worth the pixels they're written in. Go back to earning a real living." Some days, he peered at me and mocked, "That's ridiculous, what you just wrote. Who would want to read about a trip you took to a museum? You're laboring in obscurity." Or other times, "Down the rabbit hole again, are we? Checking stuff online, a style book, the *thesaurus*? Really? Even a trip downstairs to the big dictionary? Changing the font to Times New Roman, as if that will make it read any better? What a waste of time. You're just avoiding work. Which isn't worth anything anyway."

I'd always assumed I kept him because he was a memento from my mother and was a whimsical, hand-sculpted creature that sat on her desk while I was growing up. Over time, when I started to imagine him speaking to me, I also thought that he might be there to keep me humble. Humility and audacity: both necessary to creative work. But something shifted in the spring of 2021, and he seemed to gain more power than a chipped antique should.

I've never believed that "writer's block" was real; that would be like believing that if you sat at your desk long enough, the muses would float through your window and cast creative fairy dust on your fingers. I used to teach students ways to organize their writing time, how to ride the ebb and flow of work; I discouraged the notion that something "blocked" work. But this time felt—and was—different.

The semester had ended, so I should have been able to write full-time as I usually do during the break, but I was unable to do anything on my projects, even the slightest edits. Maybe I was just burned out from online teaching and the various traumas across the globe. Another week passed and another, and still, all I'd done was wander around the house, chipping away at minor writing tasks, cooking, and checking my phone too often. It wasn't the excited, slightly anxious sensation I get in starting a new project, when a brief walk or a second cup of tea, productive procrastination, helps me plunge in. It was, instead, abulia, a state of mind, from the Greek "without will, indecisiveness."

I rested my hands on the keyboard, felt a pit in my stomach, and couldn't summon even a bit of motivation. I glanced at Kappa and felt resigned to his castigations. This was not humility but something like despair. I could hear the gurgle and slurp of him dragging me into the mire.

But there is a second presence in my workspace.

Hanging on the wall just to the right of my computer screen is a postcard. It is a reproduction of an etching of Saint Anne's face, a detail from da Vinci's "The Virgin and Child with Saint

Anne and Saint John the Baptist." I bought it decades ago in the gift shop at the National Gallery in London. Her expression is soft, lightly amused. Her eyes are downcast to our right, and she gazes with benevolence out of the edge of the postcard, toward what is the Christ child in the original work. Her expression is less of awe or reverence and more loving delight, as one would have toward any child.

I am not Christian, nor do I believe in the divinity of Jesus or saints. Nevertheless, St. Anne is a guardian who ordinarily calms and motivates me.

But that late spring, when I glanced at the postcard and Kappa, I just felt annoyed. Annoyed at my private musings about saints and swamp creatures, at my fabrications of dialogues with in-animate objects. Annoyed with the hatred that streamed across our screens and airways. But those problems in the world were real. My scribblings were trivial ephemera. Kappa was winning.

Ten in the morning and I was about to give up for the day. Go fold laundry or do something else that didn't really need doing. Sprawl on the couch with a second breakfast on my lap.

And suddenly I saw Kappa as if in Saint Anne's shadow. By chance, the postcard and the figurine were positioned so that the angle of her gaze happened to skirt the top of Kappa's bald head.

Given the scale of the postcard, she loomed over him, her face twenty times the size of his.

I had always noticed the angle of her gaze toward the Child in the original etching. Indeed, she's not looking at the viewer (me) at all, as Kappa does. Yet, this angled gaze suddenly soothed me in a way that someone directly looking at me might not. Indeed, why should she look at me? For her, there is something—Someone— more important, something more compelling than my little essays and my lack of discipline. Her gentle absorption in the di-vine and the transcendent took me out of my self-absorption and, paradoxically, back to my work and what some call one's "center." It was as if she were about to laugh, a soft, musical, loving laughter ready on her lips. She knew I was there, in her peripheral vision, but was also saying, "You don't need my regard, you're fine. You need no one's regard. What you have is good."

While Saint Anne's averted eyes reflected warm compassion and gave me strength, Kappa's direct glare fed a kind of narcissistic self-denigration and anxiety that I shouldn't have indulged.

Perhaps making eye contact may not be the best strategy when we mortals comfort someone. I would think about this the next time I sat with a bereaved friend. Perhaps they would need their privacy; a direct gaze might be too strong, demand something.

Impulsively, I reached out and turned Kappa's back to me. I'd never done that, maybe superstitious that he'd unfold from his squatting stance in his squalid swamp, mince slowly over, and seek revenge. Or maybe it never occurred to me that I had that power. That I could pick him up by his spaghetti arms.

With him turned around, all I saw were his pointy elbows, his tonsured scalp, his shell. He looked more in a huff than threatening.

I smiled, less in triumph than in benignity. I am no saint, but I suspect the mirror neurons in my brain were firing as I glanced at my friend St. Anne, at her smile. Maybe the two of us felt a little sorry for Kappa.

A few days later, I turned him back around to face me. We have an understanding, I think.

21

Transition Zones

I ALWAYS IMAGINED THE MASON-DIXON LINE running horizontally east to west, straight as a student's ruler, starting at the Atlantic Ocean and fading into a midwestern blur, even though I know it was actually a jagged line. Nevertheless, when my travel companion drove us across a vertical boundary between Delaware and Maryland and announced, "Crossing into the South," I was momentarily confused. Maryland was technically the "South," at least during the Civil War, but we were driving east. My disorientation, geographic and otherwise, continued throughout that May weekend on the Eastern Shore of the Chesapeake Bay.

We soon were driving true south, past grazing horses and vast green fields of alfalfa and soybeans, interrupted only by an occasional, large farmhouse in the middle of a field. I felt soothed by the pleasant monotony of continuous green outside my window and by glimpses of the Georgian-style farmhouses with their appealing symmetry and clean trim. One house was graced with an elegant portico and a fleet of chimneys; brown furrows, as yet unplanted, surrounded it like a large corduroy blanket. But suddenly, this lovely building reminded me of the typical antebellum plantation house, and I imagined enslaved people hoeing the field. With that, my relaxation got tangled with ambivalence.

At the bed and breakfast, the innkeeper showed us our high-ceilinged cottage with its wood-burning fireplace, wing-backed chairs, and private bath adorned with fluffy bathrobes and the little toiletries I love. The grounds of the inn were dotted with lush pink peonies, purple irises, and herb gardens; enormous elm trees shaded the front lawn. It was silent except for the hum of bees.

I made lazy arcs on a long-roped swing and looked up at a blue sky through a lattice of beech leaves. In the main inn, the proprietor invited us to enjoy a stash of homemade biscotti and chewy ginger cookies any time during our stay. We perused the videos, books, and board games in the living room, and imagined returning in the winter to curl up in front of the fireplace.

In addition to a multicourse breakfast, tea was offered every afternoon, so we relaxed on the veranda and enjoyed a rich layer cake. I watched a yellow warbler peck at crumbs near our table. But I often have trouble turning off the word processor in my head, so the phrase "gracious veranda" popped to mind and conjured an image of liveried servants, slipping between the Doric columns to serve our coffee.

When I returned to the cottage, I read a brochure explaining that our room was converted from an old smokehouse.

I stopped sniffing the lavender hand cream in the bathroom and started wondering about the smokehouse. The smell of curing meat was long gone, but amid the scented toiletries and the pleasant swish of the ceiling fan was an acrid whiff of awful history: the inn had been a peach plantation dating from 1860. How could I relax in a region—a lovely region—that is haunted?

It's not that I was unaware of the history of slavery, but to my shame, that got lost in the fun and beauty of the weekend.

The next morning, after a breakfast of frittatas and crois-
sants, we drove to a wildlife refuge, an area of marsh, forest, and
meadow between the Chester River and the Chesapeake Bay.
Few people visit the park despite its rich ecology, so we had hiking trails to ourselves.

At best, I am an inept birder, but within ten minutes, I spot-
ted two bald eagles high in the trees. Then a flash of blue in my
peripheral vision—a bird flitting from marsh grass stem to cattail
before it swooped behind a screen of leaves in a swamp oak tree.
I'd just seen my first indigo bunting. Bluer than the illustrations
in the field guides, ephemeral, the sight thrilled me. Later that
day, a box turtle crunched through oak leaves beside a trail; I
marveled at the gold pattern on its black shell and the hinged
plastron. It was hot and buggy, but I felt happy.

By nine that night, most restaurants and shops in town were
closed, so we peered into the windows of galleries: a delicate,
Japanese-style screen and burnished burl-wood table in one
shop, brightly colored Italianate glass bowls in another. The local college, a small liberal arts institution, was on spring break.
Its peaceful, green quadrangles and red-brick buildings topped
with domed cupolas were reminiscent of a perfectly designed,
small-scale ivy-league campus. We strolled a new riverfront park
and the nearby quiet streets, where beautifully preserved houses
were fronted by roses and brick walkways.

Antebellum. The word on an architectural plaque startled me;
I associate it not only with a building style but also with American slavery and violence, and it shadowed my appreciation of
the town.

The waterside park was once crowded with merchants, ste-
vedores, captains, ships—and enslaved people who shaped the
bricks for the houses, sidewalks, and the college. Without slave
labor on the properties of its endowers, the college might not have
been established. And among the many "goods" passing through
the old port were exported wheat and imported human beings.

History plaques in the county do acknowledge the slave trade, and you can follow the Harriet Tubman Underground Railroad Byway, which runs through farms, natural areas, and small towns. We saw one marker next to a lily pond filled with croaking bullfrogs.

But staring at the brick buildings, I was uneasy, trying to reconcile present and past, a tourist's pleasure and a horrid history that still casts a shadow of inequity and violence in our time.

The next day, we headed to an arboretum, four hundred acres devoted to indigenous plants of the mid-Atlantic. Butterflies flitted in a wildflower meadow, and red-winged blackbirds trilled. Sweet gum, paw-paw, and persimmon trees shaded a trail dotted with pink lady slippers and jack-in-the-pulpit; a wood thrush's song fluted through the forest. Here and there, strategically fenced goats nibbled at invasive roses so that the local plants could thrive.

The arboretum displayed a healthy ecosystem—beautiful and unmanicured—the way it was before colonists clear-cut to plant hedgerows, privet, and cotton. The abundant diversity occurs because the Eastern Shore is in a "transition zone" between northern and southern natural regions, benefitting from the ecological advantages of both, and heedless of human-made boundaries and history.

Tendrils of human history reach into the present; a cruel past entwines the natural beauty and the urban charm, but nature, at least, is not intentionally cruel. In the meantime, I was trying to figure out how to be a modern visitor stepping through the whole, intricate web.

The notion of a transition zone stayed with me. Perhaps there are transition zones not only in nature but also in the liminal moments we experience in our lives: in the ambiguous, sometimes uncomfortable, sometimes sublime moments that happen between the ordinary hours.

On our last afternoon, the late day sun cast a coppery glow, its angle bringing the lines of historic buildings into crisp focus. We approached a well-maintained brick building, the County Seat, unremarkable except for two finely wrought iron benches with knobby curlicues of vines and flowers.

I read a history plaque: "On these three stone steps, African-Americans who could not pay their debts were sold into slavery."

And it hit me. The way it once did at the Holocaust Memorial Museum in Washington, DC. I grasped a hard reality, and the town's human history felt more tangible. Without realizing it, this awful reality was what I had been seeking.

Those three small steps had supported the feet of men who could be the great-great-grandfathers of a couple strolling the waterfront path or eating ice cream in the town square. They lived, worked, had families, and couldn't pay their debts.

On those steps, humans sold other humans.

I kneeled, put my palm on the cold granite, and had an unanticipated urge. Searching in a well-tended shade garden on the grounds, I dug my fingers into the dirt under the azaleas, but there wasn't one rock, not even a piece of gravel.

I wanted a stone like the ones that Jews put on graves to mark a visit. The granite steps were like the grave markers of the men who were sold there, and I wanted to signal that I'd been there, even if I didn't know their names.

When I approached the steps again, empty-handed, I noticed something. In the quiet of the park, on the second step, was a figurine, maybe two inches high. It was a toy football player in a blue-and-white uniform, his arm drawn back to pass a tiny football. His plastic skin was brown. He perched there, still and small, making a little shadow.

I moved it slightly as though this little statue might stand in for something like a visitation stone on a grave.

We will perhaps never—should never—find a way to reconcile the cruelty of our country's history with its beauty, but we still must mark our visits, say that we were here, with the whispers of history and the caw of the jay. We cannot reconcile the past, but in continuing the effort, in facing the truth of the past, in teaching it, in remembering, and in accepting that we will never complete this struggle—that is a ritual that might mean something.

22

Spreading Out

WHEN THE CHILDREN WERE SIX AND NINE, my children's father and I decided to legally separate and start the divorce process. We sat with them on the blue couch in the living room and explained that their dad was moving to a different house a few blocks away. They would live in both houses on a rotating schedule.

"But I don't want you to do that! Then it'll be Mommy's house and Daddy's house, not our house," Noah said, gesturing to Chrys and himself. He started crying. Chrys didn't say anything but looked as if they were trying to puzzle it out.

Noah begged us to continue the arrangement we'd kept for two and a half years, what is sometimes called "nesting custody." The children stayed put in the house while we took equal turns in a nearby rental apartment and the house. Although their parents didn't live together, the children were in their familiar home, and we attended their birthday parties, soccer games, choir concerts, and school conferences together. Whoever was in the apartment called to say good-night; I sang each child's favorite lullaby over the phone. We kept the schedule on a bulletin board in the kitchen at the house.

Chrys had called that first arrangement "spreading out." We didn't correct them, and I never knew if they had misunderstood

the word "separating," or if this is how it felt—like their world had
expanded rather than split in two. And our nesting custody did
seem less upsetting than many marital separations I'd witnessed.
Perhaps it was less disruptive; we were taking care of them in the
same place we always had, just separately. They didn't have to
contend with a move or a new place along with the separation.
Moreover, we rarely disagreed about the children; our child-rear-
ing beliefs and practices were similar. And we kept the real con-
flicts out of sight. So, the first phase of the separation had been a
difficult change but probably not a traumatic one. For them, that
is. I missed them terribly when I was at the apartment, especially
during the first year. In an odd way, Chrys's term "spreading out"
had comforted me.

As we sat on the couch, Noah stopped crying and asked about
the schedule, where the house was, how we'd manage their clothes
and toys. We showed the children a black gym bag we'd use to
carry their favorite stuffed animals, school notebooks, whatever
book they were reading, and other necessities. They'd have plenty
of clothes, toys, and supplies at both houses, and they were free
to stop by either house any time they wanted to. I knew that, on
some level, these reassurances were for us as well as the children:
having two permanent residences signaled a finality, a realization
that the family was never going back to the way it was. And we
were legalizing the separation. This went beyond spreading out.

The questions wound down. We hugged the children and sat
quietly.

Chrys suddenly sat up straight and looked at each of us. In
their face, I saw something they had given voice to a few years
before. They'd fallen from the top of the monkey bars on the
playground, onto a padded surface. I imagine it hurt, but Chrys
said, "Don't comfort me yet." I remember that toddler with the
set jaw and quietly fierce voice.

But separation and divorce were no playground mishap.

In a matter-of-fact tone, Chrys asked, "Can I name the houses?"

"Name the houses?" I repeated.

"Yes," they said, "Can I name the houses?" Of course, we replied.

Sometimes time really does seem to slow. Sometimes we know we are witnessing something profound. This was one of those times.

Chrys nodded. "Okay," they said brightly, "Dad's house will be 'Little House on the Prairie,' and Mom's will be 'the Castle.'"

I do not know if Chrys had been working this out the whole time, but no therapist could have devised such an intervention.

Naming. We name a child, we have baby-naming ceremonies, we recite the names of the deceased on the anniversary of death. We change our own names to mark transitions. And we "name" worries and fears and, in doing so, diminish them.

A name has incantatory power, and the names Chrys had chosen seemed not only rooted in their childish imagination and literary world but also in the meaning of these homes. Dad's Little House on the Prairie was new territory, a place ripe for exploration, a place full of unknowns. The children didn't know yet, but the house was also at the edge of woods—not a geographic prairie, but as close to untamed wilderness as our urban neighborhood had to offer. It was also "little," smaller than the house they'd known their whole lives.

And the Castle? The house was a three-story, stone building that must have seemed endlessly tall to a young child. A fortress, perhaps, against unseen threats, a place of safety. A place where a miniature battalion of wizards, dragons, knights, mermaids, and princesses on horseback stood guard on Chrys's window-sill. Fairies brandished swords, and unicorns kept watch. The figurines had been collected and lined up over the years, for fun, surely, but perhaps also as amulets against the dark outside the window. The figures made their way into our bedtime stories.

Elfin tales and swashbuckling adventures always ended with, "And they came back to their bed and went ... to ... sleep." It was our lights-out mantra.

In other rooms, more magic and royalty: costume gowns and capes for any fancy occasion, plastic swords, shields, armor and helmets, wizards' and witches' hats, magic wands to cast spells. Room for dancing and music, for perching on deep window sills and looking out on the tops of trees, for birthday parties with buried treasures and princely decor, and all kinds of fêtes through the seasons.

There was even a dungeon—the basement—where dark corners and shadows and occasional squeaks and rustles hinted at the unknown living in that damp place.

Outside, the children and their friends brewed potions of herbs, leaves, and flowers; picked apples and wild mint; sipped nectar from honeysuckle blossoms.

Chrys's names for the houses seemed prescient, especially because they hadn't seen their dad's house yet. There was also some unintended humor. Although the children's blocks, miniature trains, tiny dolls, and crayons littered the floor in most rooms, I was a careful housekeeper, and my home was maybe a bit formal. In their dad's little house on the prairie, housekeeping was more casual, and dusty antiques, dried-out wreaths, rocks, and books and papers jumbled together in most rooms. Old wicker chairs, conch shells, and household discards sat comfortably together on the covered porch, while projects like fermenting sauerkraut or drying herbs adorned the kitchen counters. As important, the woods across the street and the novelty of the home could be an adventure, like on a prairie.

These qualities and connotations occurred to me later. What impressed me in that moment on the couch was the act itself. My small child had named the unknown, the future, something out of their control. It was a moment of awe.

As for my son's worry about the houses not being his and Chrys's, we suggested that he call them both "his" houses, not Mom's and Dad's. He was skeptical.

But the children adjusted more quickly than I had anticipated. They were soon packing up the black bag on the changeover mornings, or running back for a sweatshirt they wanted. They'd ask, "Am I at Dad's tonight?" more as a practical than an emotional matter. As they got older, we simplified the schedule and stopped trying to keep the days even between the houses. The children occasionally asked to be at Dad's because they wanted help with science homework or Mom's because they wanted a sleepover with friends, with more space. But mostly, they stuck to the schedule because it was easier not to have to figure it out every week.

Perhaps they adjusted quickly and well because we'd already been separated for three years. Perhaps because both houses were a few minutes apart, in the familiar neighborhood where most of their friends lived. Perhaps it was our lack of conflict about the custody arrangement that made it easier.

Or maybe, it was Chrys's ritual naming of the Little House and the Castle that helped. Although, after that day on the blue couch, I never heard those names again.

23

Love in the Time of COVID

MY FAMILY RECEIVED A "SAVE THE DATE" CARD in December 2019 from my nephew and his fiancée announcing their marriage for the July Fourth weekend the following year in Colombia, where Ana's family was from. My extended family was thrilled and planned to travel from Seattle, Boston, London, and many points between. Given the young couple's exuberance, I anticipated an elegant, busy weekend.

The photo card, which I still have on my kitchen bulletin board, shows the couple with their arms around each other—John, fair-haired, lightly freckled, with a confident smile, and Ana, her long hair draped over one shoulder and a manicured left hand showing a sparkling engagement ring.

When he was a toddler, John had ventured confidently into new territory, whether climbing a tree or skateboarding or learning karate. As an adult, he dived into the real estate business with equal aplomb and enjoyment. The wedding plans were no different. Over the next few months, he and Ana created a webpage that sprouted more and more celebratory details, all written with an enthusiasm I recognized. Soon, we were invited to book hotels and started to look forward to hikes, sight-seeing, an elegant rehearsal dinner, gorgeous wedding venue, and places to hang out together.

Our large extended family would likely attend, along with the couple's friends from around the country. Despite some challenging travel logistics, it would be worth it. Not only was John the first among his cousins to get married, but many in our family believed this about happy rituals: "Just go, if you can; you won't regret it." And John's mother, my oldest sister, kept crowing, "I'm going to be a mother-in-law!" We would be there to support and celebrate.

I booked my tickets early and prodded my children to do the same. We discussed when we'd arrive, maybe squeeze in some extra touring in Colombia; when else might we get the chance? Besides, it was important to Ana and John to be married in her home country; we'd have a family reunion; and, judging from the social schedule, it looked like a six-costume-change weekend, so I'd get to dress up, something I enjoy but rarely get to do. I started planning outfits and considered getting new shoes. I love these adornments to ritual; they are frivolous but, like flowers and music and dancing, add to the delight of ceremonies and enhance the sense of importance.

The number of texts and phone calls increased as we all compared notes about flights, how to get my elderly mother to Medellin, and which cousins might attend. The couple kept us up-to-date on venues, menus, and additional touring recommendations. Ana chose a dress, the two of them put down deposits for the festivities, and my mother was excited about the impending "nuptials" and mentioned it every time we spoke. Soon, the couple started planning a honeymoon, and the mother-in-law-to-be regularly sent photos of possible dresses, flowers, Colombian locales.

Late winter, two unrelated things happened in the same week. John and Ana sent out their formal wedding invitations by surface mail, and a viral wave surged across the world.

Three days after the engaged couple mailed their last invitation, the country went on lockdown.

In March, John and Ana debated delaying the wedding to the summer or perhaps fall. But as spring wore on, streets emptied, and theaters and restaurants shut down. A gloomy anxiety saturated our days and our dreams.

They considered a wedding in their backyard, with only their parents attending. Encouraged by that prospect Ana bought a simple, inexpensive dress online, foregoing the elaborate gown she'd planned. But as they started planning, even a mini-wedding seemed complicated: what about toilet facilities? a food buffet? It all seemed too risky. And Ana's stepfather lived in New Jersey, with travel impossible. Eventually, they told us they were postponing indefinitely but were philosophical about the decision and were committed to each other. John and Ana were not alone in their decision; most large gatherings then were canceled.

I arranged a refund for my ticket to Medellin.

Sometime later, I received a text from John saying they were driving north to visit Ana's stepfather, who had fallen ill, and asking if they could stop by briefly at my house on the first Saturday of June. I was delighted. My children were home and my niece lived in town, so we could have a small reunion.

When they appeared at my front walk, I teared up; it had been months since I'd seen extended family. We had some snacks and iced tea; they caught us up on family, work, their garden, and other light news. The young adult cousins were particularly happy to hang out with each other.

After a time, John and Ana shared an enigmatic smile. "We have some news," John grinned and paused to look at each of us. Ana nodded to him, encouraging him to continue. "We got married!"

The congratulations, whoops, and questions tumbled across the porch, and they proceeded to tell a tale I would repeat again and again in the coming months.

On Wednesday, May 20, 2020, they woke up and said, "Let's get married—today." Late morning, they began calling around. No answer at the elegant Presbyterian church. They drove over, but it was empty, the door locked. They called another local church, who said they could come the following week, but the fee was high, and besides, the couple wanted it to be that day. They checked other places online without luck. At the Catholic church, they roamed from building to building until they found a priest who told them he'd be able to officiate. That is, after the customary six-month marriage preparation course and counseling.

In the parking lot of the church, John and Ana deliberated and then remembered a place they'd considered the previous year, before deciding to get married in Medellin. When they called the Ancient Spanish Monastery, Pastor Greg took their call. "How is three thirty this afternoon?" he asked, "Chapel or garden courtyard?" They opted for the courtyard, which was peaceful, green, and less expensive. The monastery had been converted to an Episcopal church, but like its name, it was a reconstruction of a twelfth-century Spanish monastery, using the original stones. The monastery had come to Florida via Brooklyn, New York, where the building materials had sat in crates after William Randolph Hearst had illegally purchased and shipped the deconstructed church to the US. He'd wanted it for his own use in California. That never happened.

John and Ana had just over an hour to get ready. They raced home from the church parking lot, snarfed some crackers, cheese, chocolate, and red wine. Ana hastily washed and styled her hair and did her makeup, threw on informal sandals and the simple white dress that she had ordered online. But as John donned a sports coat over a pair of jeans, they realized they hadn't purchased wedding rings yet. Ana could use her engagement ring for the ceremony, but John had nothing.

In the garage of their house, he sifted through shelves of supplies and grabbed a spool of soldering wire. Taking an approximated length, he twisted it into a crisscross pattern, looped it around his finger, and squeezed the makeshift ring together to fit securely on his finger.

From their car, they called the pastor to say they would be twenty minutes late. "By the way," John asked, "The church wouldn't happen to know a photographer we could call last minute?" The pastor had told them no one was around except for him, a secretary, and a custodian. "But hold on," he said over the phone. A congregant had stopped by for some reason—a congregant who happened to be a professional photographer—and he was standing right in front of Pastor Greg. "Tell him to wait!" Ana said over the phone.

As they started to drive, it began to pour with what some call "Miami monsoons." They could barely see out the windows. They cranked up the windshield wipers and an upbeat jazzy tune, the one they'd originally planned as their wedding song: "Adventure of a Lifetime."

It was still pouring when they arrived at the monastery. The custodian was sweeping water from the walkways with a large broom, and Ana's sandals and the hem of her dress were soaked as they scooted into the church offices.

They stood dripping in the reception area with the secretary, pastor, and photographer and then chatted with Pastor Greg for a few minutes about how they met, their work together, and a bit about family. The small group looked out at the rainy courtyard, now unsuitable with its sodden ground and deep puddles. The pastor, already in his white vestments with purple trim, smiled briefly and offered them the chapel at the same rate as the courtyard. The small chapel had thick stone walls and a modest altar, with two tiny rose windows providing a soft natural light. The windows had somehow survived the centuries, the dismantling of the monastery, and a trans-Atlantic crossing. The couple happily accepted his offer.

Ana looked at John. "We didn't get any flowers," she said. "Oh, well." But the secretary signaled them to wait and, returning from an adjoining room, handed Ana a fresh, sumptuous bouquet of white flowers dotted with small pink roses, held in a rubber band and wrapped in brown paper towels. "This arrived at the office today for us," she said. "Why don't you take it?"

In the chapel, John and the pastor stood in front of the altar, with the photographer off to the side. Ana waited outside the closed door of the chapel in a covered breezeway and, without a mirror, neatened her hair. The secretary opened the door for her, and in silence, she walked slowly down the aisle, her fresh bouquet, freed from its paper towels, glowing in the dim light of the two small windows of the medieval church.

The pastor proceeded to give a brief introduction to the ceremony, highlighting the couple's personal history, how they met, and their attachment to one another. He commented on their rings. "It was all unbelievable, as if he knew us," John told me later. The pastor's words were based only on the casual, brief conversation earlier in the day.

After the simple vows, John put Ana's engagement ring back on her finger, and Ana slipped the homemade soldering wire loop onto John's.

When the group opened the door to leave the chapel, sunlight poured in. The storm was over. The photographer posed the newlyweds embracing among bright red flowers, jumping in unison along a path, and kissing beneath an ancient arch.

They hadn't even told their parents yet.

A quick stop at Walgreens after the ceremony yielded bottles of champagne, sparkling cider, and some plastic cups. They called Ana's mother, Gloria, who lived with Ana's *abuela* (grandmother), saying they wanted to drop something off.

When John pulled up, Ana hid behind a pillar outside the entrance. Gloria and Abuela came out, masks on their faces, disposable blue gloves covering their hands. They greeted John, and he glanced surreptitiously at Ana, peaking behind the pillar. She walked out slowly, filming on her phone. The women took in the dress and flowers and started jumping up and down, clapping and exclaiming. "*Se casaron*?!" her mother cried out. "*Si*," said Ana, "*Nos casamos*!" (Did you get married?! Yes, we got married.)

The apartment building abutted the bay, coppery and blue in the late afternoon light. The four family members gathered at the seawall, took pictures and shared champagne as the newlyweds told Gloria and Abuela the story of their wedding.

John and Ana posed for some selfies and started to leave. They walked along the seawall, holding the champagne and flowers and waving good-bye to the two women, but a sound coming from the apartment building made them stop and turn around. On a third-floor balcony of the building stood a man with a violin tucked under his chin and his bow drawing across the strings. Expert strains of "La Vie en Rose" drifted across the late afternoon. John placed the open champagne bottle and the bouquet on the grass and held his arms out to Ana for their first dance, en plein air. Soon, other apartment dwellers came onto their balconies, watching, clapping, and calling congratulations. Even the sunset cooperated in its timing, providing a rich backdrop to their dance and a kiss. After dancing for a bit, they stopped and calculated in which apartment the violinist was living. Another person on the balcony gestured at his phone: he'd been filming, and with shouts, hand gestures, and texts, they exchanged numbers with the amateur videographer and the professional violinist. That image of their first dance, which they later shared, was more gorgeous than any polished wedding video.

Next stop was John's dad's house, with the same routine of Ana hiding and filming and John saying he wanted to drop something off. It was dark by then, but the film shows a flabbergasted but proud and smiling dad shaking his head in disbelief. The three celebrated briefly in the backyard, and the couple soon got back into the car.

Last stop, John's mother, my sister Abbie. On the way, they ordered pizza with panna cotta for dessert from O'Munaciello's on Biscayne Boulevard, then called my sister to ask if she'd like to meet them in the backyard for pizza.

Same routine, same hiding, same filming, and same reaction by the second mom: confusion, half questions, astonished revelation, and happy gasps and tears. In the dark, they ate and toasted, took pictures, and Ana and John related the day's tale. "Hold on," Abbie said, "I want to get something." She came back with a tiny box and handed it to Ana. It was Abbie's old engagement ring, a perfect complement to Ana's, and could serve as the second official ring on her finger. Ana told me it mostly fit, and she wore it for a long time.

After the panna cotta, the newlyweds took an early leave; they were happy but exhausted.

At their two-year anniversary, in May 2022, they finally took their honeymoon, a romp through Italy and France.

In the months following their tale on my front porch, I found myself reading wedding reports in the newspaper, something I rarely had done. The back stories, from all over the country, had a similar pattern: we had invited 150 people . . . we had a guest list of 300 . . . a destination wedding in Aruba . . . we rented a large hall and garden venue . . . a four-course dinner was planned . . . the caterer, DJ, and wedding planner were all booked."

The actual weddings in the reports also followed a pattern: we ended up in our front yard with a small barbecue and homemade brownies . . . we got married at the public park down the street . . . only our parents and siblings attended . . . our neighbors came out and watched and cheered from across the street . . . we used flowers from our garden . . . my brother became a temporary minister . . . we took the money we would have spent on the big wedding and donated it. Couples in the stories repeated, "We realized what was important, what was essential."

And in south Florida, in one small moment, a small group of strangers and a family made a wedding and a party out of nothing, and in its simplicity, in its serendipity, something angelic arose, something that defied the demons of the world, something that was playful and meaningful and precious.

We fragile humans need these spontaneous, simple rituals as much as the planned, elaborate ones. Even in the time of COVID, life could sparkle like champagne, like a diamond.

24

The Toolbox and the Ring

JUST BECAUSE A RITUAL HAS ROOTS running deep into the past doesn't automatically confer substance. In fact, one can stumble upon newer rituals that contain more meaning. I learned this after my second marriage.

At my first divorce, I had asked my rabbi what to do with the ketubah, the Jewish marriage contract. Ours was a poster-sized, calligraphed parchment with hand-painted leaves and flowers in fall colors. The rabbi shrugged. "You bury it," he said. Some sacred documents that are defective or nullified are buried in a special kind of grave because holy texts can't just be thrown in the trash with dirty paper towels and onion peels. That wasn't the answer I was looking for. It made sense to treat a sacred parchment with respect, and maybe a rule against discarding it in the trash prevents some people from ripping to shreds everything associated with a distasteful marriage or divorce. But I couldn't do it. Burial seemed too stark; I couldn't take something so beautiful, a piece of art really, and just cover it with dirt. My first husband, David, suggested we donate the ketubah to a Jewish museum, but I didn't want this very personal object on display. I didn't want the document—or us—to be relics. The rabbi didn't suggest an alternative.

So, the ketubah sat in my home office for a decade until I was about to get married a second time. As my fiancé, Tim, and I planned our wedding, I felt the need to put a punctuation mark on my first marriage.

One weekend morning, I pulled out the old wedding album and the invitation, a scrap of lace from my wedding dress (the dress had been my mother's), the wedding ring, a place card, typed vows, and some other objects. We looked at all of it together, stowed the album on a high bookshelf, removed the ketubah from its frame, rolled it tightly, and stowed and locked all the mementos inside a gray, steel toolbox, which had the perhaps not incidental appearance of a miniature casket. Tim climbed the rickety, pull-down steps to the attic and placed the steel case among the old furniture and boxes with unknown contents. It felt like I had turned a page.

The little casket sat there for more than twenty-five years. I never looked at it. Sometimes, I wondered if pests may have gotten to it, and I wasn't sure where the key was, but no matter. I suppose it was akin to entombment in a mausoleum, and a kind of burial that I ultimately found acceptable. I knew it was there, but it felt final. Remembered, but gone.

Once in a while, though, I thought the rabbi may have been right. Perhaps I should have buried the ketubah in the earth. Interment of such a document treats these sacred pages as more than paper and ink and is consistent with Jewish custom regarding old Torah scrolls. These were once living documents but are no longer viable, so burial has a metaphoric resonance. Sometimes when I thought about it, I liked the idea of that marriage parchment gradually disintegrating in the earth, forming compost for trees or flowers, transforming a holy object into part of nature. Nevertheless, the toolbox in the attic seemed to do its ritualistic job.

It turns out, though, that the divorce rites weren't over. A few years after my second wedding, I heard from David, who said

he had a request, but I was under no obligation. He was getting remarried, and would I attend a *get* with him? The get is an
ancient Jewish legal ceremony that nullifies the obligations of
marriage. The word *get* also refers to the associated document.
I was happy to.

I met him at a nondescript building in midtown Manhattan
and took the elevator to a nondescript office. We were ushered
to a room lined with heavy, black-leather-bound Jewish books
and were seated at a long wooden table opposite a severe, bored-
looking Orthodox rabbi.

The ceremony began with prayers and what seemed like incantations, delivered rapid and pro forma in the cadences I'd
come to associate with some religious services and long-gone
great uncles from Eastern Europe. The whole thing probably took
forty-five minutes, but I honestly can't remember much about the
ceremony except the following.

David is civil but also funny, so before the ceremony, he had
whispered a somewhat sardonic view of part of the ritual; those
comments, more than the proceedings that followed, made it
hard to keep a straight face. And when David responded to the
rabbi's questions and repeated the ceremonial phrases, his voice
probably sounded appropriate to those listening, but I recognized in it his subtly ironic undertone.

I could not take the ritual seriously, and although that may
seem disrespectful, it was probably because I didn't buy into the
idea that a wife was a possession and the husband the possessor.
In fact, I learned later that when David was instructed to actually
hand me the get, a central part of the ceremony, he was fulfill-
ing a religious legal requirement that would "release" me from
the marriage. And it turns out the string of words he was told
to repeat in Hebrew when handing me the get (the rabbi didn't
translate), meant, "You are hereby permitted to all men." Yuck! I
was, according to Jewish law, now free to marry and apparently,
available to all takers. Again, yuck.

Despite my amusement, I could not help feeling uncomfortable with the sexism. But I also found myself somewhat obsessed with the fact that I was wearing a shiny, relatively new gold wedding band. I kept my hand in my lap.

Was it kosher to be getting the Jewish divorce *after* I'd married under civil law—and indeed, by a rabbi, with yet another ketubah? Turns out, no. According to Jewish law, I'd technically been committing adultery for two years, since there'd been no get before my remarriage. I had this image of a second rabbi bursting into the room, shouting, "Stop the proceedings! Adulteress! Bigamist! Harlot!"

But the peremptory way in which the rabbi raced through the ceremony suggested he would not be likely to scrutinize my left hand nor call for halachic police assistance.

In the end, the event seemed very much as if we had just made a real estate transaction, with me being the real property. Come to think of it, the two times I've bought houses, there was more gravitas and warmth, more of a sense of an important transition. Almost ritualistic.

It's not that I would have rejected the idea of fully and sincerely participating in a get; I like the idea of a ritual associated with a divorce. In the US, at least, the secular divorce process is often adversarial, with legal and financial processes that can be soul killing and harmful to relationships. While the get has a legal foundation in Judaism, it also contains a religious and ceremonial element, and there is a modern version that is egalitarian without implying a woman is a chattel requiring permission to remarry.

I was sort of sorry that the get wasn't like that. Our divorce had been a secular-legal matter that ended when we signed the papers: no ritualized marker of a shift in status or opportunity for emotional reflection. By the time we had that orthodox get, I felt no lingering unfinished emotional business, but at the time of the legal divorce, I remember wanting something meaningful, something rooted in Judaism, something that acknowledged the very real commitment we had during part of the marriage, as well as the dissolution of it. This get wasn't that. I was only doing it as a courtesy to my first husband and his fiancée.

But I'd had my moment with the steel casket. And two years later, something unexpected occurred, something that served as a coda to the first marriage's faint melody.

For our engagement, David and I had chosen a platinum ring adorned with a diminutive, deep-blue sapphire between two tiny diamonds. I always loved the rich color of the sapphire, which changed with the light; the diamonds enhanced the sapphire, and in sunshine, they acted as prisms, sending tiny rainbows shimmering along white tablecloths or windowsills. During our marriage, I frequently wore it with my wedding ring. The ring was the most beautiful piece of jewelry I owned.

I'd developed the habit of using my left thumb to touch the engagement ring on my left ring finger, at first to make sure it hadn't slipped off, but also, I'd learned to flip it around with the thumb when on a busy bus or train, so that all you saw was the silvery band. Perhaps it was overcautious, but I didn't want to lose it. And it became a meaningless, maybe soothing habit.

But after the divorce, I stopped wearing both rings. I couldn't bring myself to don the sapphire as a mere piece of fancy jewelry, so it sat undisturbed in its little satin-lined, hinged case. It sat because, while beautiful as adornment, there was also meaning that lingered in the solid gemstones, the shiny platinum. From time to time, the knowledge of its existence in my possession weighed on me.

At a party one day, the wife of an acquaintance suggested turning my ring into a pin or earrings. "See?" she said and lifted a lovely pendant resting at her throat. "This," she said with some pride, "is what I did with the engagement ring from my first marriage."

But that wasn't for me. A jeweler's redesign of the piece wouldn't impart emotional or spiritual transformation; the ring would always hold its original meaning. Rituals with an object like an engagement imbue the object with meaning that is carried forward. And I couldn't pass it down to my children; that felt wrong. But I also couldn't bring myself to sell it. Perhaps it was a last symbolic remnant of the promise of that first marriage, even though the promise had withered; it was a reminder that the marriage had been substantive, the emotions real, even though it all ended. But unlike shriveled marriages, diamonds, sapphires, and platinum unsentimentally keep their form and sparkle. Like the toolbox, the ring was out of sight, but unlike the toolbox, it was not in its final resting place. In truth, too, the ring was exquisite, and I wasn't ready to part with it, even though I never wore it anymore. So, it sat.

But a few years into my second marriage, I was ready to sell it and got in touch with the original jeweler. He said he'd be happy to meet and was charmed to hear that I'd retained the original receipt, so old that it was handwritten with a carbon copy. I'd also had the ring appraised and shared that information with him.

The morning of my appointment, I met an old friend at the American Museum of Natural History in New York, where we meandered in the dim light among the massive Easter Island statues and under the model of the great blue whale, which seemed to float over the echo of voices. In the hall of gems and minerals, iridescent and luminescent stones cast spells in our wake.

At a sidewalk cafe on the Upper West Side, we caught up on our family news and talked easily, as always. She was bemused by my planned mission for the afternoon and dutifully admired both the ring and my fortitude.

Throughout the trip, I'd worn the ring on my left hand as I had years before, figuring it was safer than transporting it in my handbag or a pocket. I found myself automatically and frequently flicking it with my thumb in the old habitual way.

Later that day, I took an elevator in yet another unremarkable office building. I'd been told the address and given instructions:

for security, there was no sign for the business: not on the building, nor on the lobby directory or on the designated floor. I was
to proceed directly to the proper floor and bring no one with me.
As I got off the elevator, it was silent. The jeweler was apparently
the only office on the floor.

Three solid walls were interrupted only by the elevator door
and, embedded in the fourth wall was a locked, glass-encased vestibule, like a large version of Snow White's casket. As instructed, I
rang a buzzer, and a man I thought I recognized entered the glass
enclosure. A door behind him closed automatically, and through
heavy glass, he seemed to appraise my identity as closely as he
might a carat weight. I thought I might have to answer a series
of three wizard's questions. Then he smiled and let me into the
enclosure with him. The door clicked and locked behind me, and
only then did the interior door to the offices open. Did I imagine
that he whispered something akin to *abracadabra*? I felt a rush
of air. We entered, and the door locked itself behind us. Sanctum
sanctorum.

The jeweler led me through a quiet, narrow hallway past an
unmarked door. Further on, pure white light streamed from an
open room. I caught a glimpse: a row of silent men bent over a
long table dotted with tweezers, files, pliers. Some wore jeweler's
loupes, others, magnifying visors, and in the custom of some Orthodox Jewish sects, all were bearded, with long side curls, black
skullcaps, black vests, white shirts, and tzitzits (prayer fringes)
that fluttered at their hips. It was an elves' workshop run by a
yeshivah. Before I could fully take in the twinkle of gems on the
table, the jeweler steered me firmly by the elbow down the silent
hall. At the third door, he entered a code on a keypad, and we
entered a windowless conference room.

At times, there may be a fine line between the mystical, the
sacred, and the profane. Gemstones figure large in fairy tales:
they signal the entrance to a secret or magical place; they are
traded for promises, firstborns, and souls; holding them can

impart special powers, and hurling them into a void can be cata-strophic or liberating. Ogres and dragons protect troves of jew-els; wizards imbue precious metals and gems with magic that is sometimes sweet, sometimes dark. Perhaps the workers in that bright room instilled not only technical and aesthetic excellence in their pieces but also probity or even magic charm: after all, some of the jewelry was destined for engagements, weddings, and other rituals requiring more than cold elements of the earth, shaped by human hands.

The conference room was silent as a dragon's lair.

On the walls were glossy, framed photos of brooches, neck-laces, and earrings that could count as weight-lifting equipment, if you preferred yours with bling. In one picture, a regal member of the glitterati beguiled us with a familiar face that had launched quite a few ships. Her eyes sparkled like sapphires above dazzling diamond earrings and a heavy diamond necklace.

The jeweler sat opposite me at the table, greeted me warmly, and asked after my family. I soon placed the receipt and appraisal on the table. "May I see the ring?" he asked. I twisted it off my finger and handed it to him. He secured a loupe against his eye. "It's in good condition," he said, looking up. "There was that one repair," I noted. "Yes," he said, "I can see a trace of it." A few weeks after my first wedding, I'd noticed a hairline crack in the metal. At the time, the jeweler had been surprised that I had noticed the tiny break but repaired it gratis. I could not help wondering later if that nearly invisible flaw was an omen for my short-lived marriage.

He handed the ring back to me. "It's a sweet ring," he said, with an indulgent smile. "Have you considered selling it yourself?" he added.

I was flustered. Somehow, I had thought we were beginning a transaction; besides, I didn't have a clue how to sell real jewelry, online or otherwise.

He held his hand out for the ring and examined it again. In the bright light of that room, it gleamed and sparkled as if the stones and metal were emitting light. It was one of those quiet moments where you feel things can go any direction, what philosophers call *limina*, between two states. I was half expecting him to perform some sort of alchemy or perhaps we'd be tele-transported.

"To be honest, I'm afraid we don't really sell this sort of piece anymore," he said, "Though it's very pretty." He was, clearly, doing me a favor.

He handed me back the ring a second time. "We have two choices," he said. "I can put it up for consignment, as is, with one of my dealers, but our name won't be on a piece that's this . . . modest, so it won't go for as much." "Can you give me a ballpark?" I asked. And he named a dollar amount that was about a quarter of what the ring had been most recently appraised.

"Or," he continued, "as is more common in cases like this and more favorable for you, we would extract the gems and perhaps use them in a larger piece. Or sell them with other lots." My hand tightened around the ring, but I extended it to him a third time.

Suddenly, I imagined a phantom circle of buxom divas and majestic movie stars shimmering around us: meteoric tiaras on their towering coiffures, supernova brooches arrayed on their chests, glittering waterfalls of gems cascading from their earlobes, and my three little stones providing a barely discernible shimmer in a universe of diamonds.

"And the setting?" I asked tentatively. The phantom divas had disappeared, and another image hovered in the corners, like black spreading shadows in the bright light.

"Oh, we just sell jewelry scraps like that in lots or, very rarely," he said, "use it for our own repairs. It depends." He smiled pleasantly, placed the ring on a black velvet pad, and adjusted the cuffs of his white shirt.

Despite the comfortable room, I felt a chill. I imagined my ring without its three snug stones, the delicate prongs twisted, their gems wrenched from their protective grasp. I saw heaps of such empty settings, sad empty pieces, tangled with bent wedding rings and broken pieces of white and yellow gold, platinum, silver, all in piles waiting to be sorted and melted down, contorted, and unceremoniously heaped like the detritus of failed marriages or of deaths without heirs or financial ruin that required the pawning of heirlooms. And my little ring setting, minus its minuscule weights, would be tossed onto that heap, with a faint tinkling sound as the pile shifted. And worse, in my imagination, that gleaming mass of empty, pronged rings, soon was shoveled into an even larger pile, a haunting, horrible image that I'd seen in black-and-white photographs of sorted property looted from victims of the Holocaust.

"What do you think?" he asked, and the ghosts fled the room. "I would reappraise the ring and send you an exact price. If at that point you'd like to pursue an alternative, I'd be happy to send it back to you, insured at our expense."

I regained my composure. I believe he had seen none of the apparitions. "Oh, of course, yes, definitely, that sounds good."

I left the building, knowing he would offer a more than fair deal, but it had all happened so quickly that I felt disoriented and, for a moment, couldn't figure out which was uptown and which downtown.

As I stood getting my bearings, out of nowhere I felt as if the ring was back on my hand. I truly felt its delicate weight, the familiar sense of slight pressure around my finger, and I intuitively flicked my thumb, as if spinning the ring.

Even as I glanced at my hand, feeling a little silly and knowing it was, by now, locked away in the offices above, the sensation lingered.

It likely lasted seconds, but it felt like minutes, and then, the feeling vanished. No barely perceptible weight on my finger, no hard metal, no rub of a faceted stone.

The closest I can describe the feeling was like a phantom limb sensation, as if the ring had been a physical part of me and now was gone.

As a rational person and trained psychologist, I hope I can distinguish between the transient sensation of a tactile memory—which this was—and frank tactile hallucinations, which this was not. But the tiny wraith that briefly lit on my finger and flew seemed more than a neuro-perceptual phenomenon. It was a suitably charmed ending.

25

Kedushah

MY MOTHER-IN-LAW, LIZ, called at seven on a Wednesday morning in June to tell us Tom, her husband, died in the night. "I woke up early, maybe four o'clock," she said, "And it was quiet; he was not in bed. I assumed he had come to sleep after me, but perhaps he never did. And then I found him," she added. "In the bathroom. I called the doctor. The people from the funeral home are coming at ten."

On the drive to her house, I wept briefly; I would tend to my grief later, after I told my children that their paternal grandfather had died.

When we arrived, phones rang in and out: the transport, the funeral home, medical office. The family was reviewing Tom's wish to be cremated. And amid this, my brother-in-law was to be married in two weeks. They calmly discussed the logistics, the practical concerns. They weighed the options. "Shouldn't we wait to have the funeral until after the wedding?" they were saying.

"No," I interrupted. "We have to bury him first." Certainty rose in me unmediated by deliberation. How else would we have some semblance of joy if this hung over us? We needed to mourn, then celebrate unencumbered by the anticipation of having to bury a father. There would be plenty of time to grieve.

Although I am not particularly observant in daily life, I found myself intuitively calling upon the Jewish tradition of quick burial. Perhaps ritual comes not only from belief but also from the needs of the human psyche.

The family was Quaker, with few ritualistic guideposts and few mitzvot (religious duties), as Jewish families may have. I was moved by how thoughtful they were in planning, but their shock and sadness seemed unframed.

In the end, they decided the burial would be within a week, before the wedding, and a memorial service would follow in the fall. My mother-in-law agreed but was preoccupied with something.

"There is one thing I would like to ask you to do, if you're willing," she said to me privately. "The funeral home put me in touch with a cleaning service." She was usually so articulate, her voice strong. That day it wavered, and she searched for words: "The bathroom . . ."

I waited.

"They would like to know," she said, "Generally, they need . . . someone to look and tell them. I can't. I only glanced in the semi-darkness this morning and called the medics right away." She could not say any more.

"I'll talk to them," I said. "I'll go and look."

When I called the cleaning service, they asked me to estimate the dimensions of the bathroom and the extent and kind of "biomedical waste." That term in 2007—and years later—veiled so much suffering. I told them I'd look and would call back.

With more grief than worry, I mounted the stairs.

When we'd arrived at the house earlier that morning, they were just removing Tom's body enclosed in a zipped black vinyl bag on a wheeled gurney. I wanted them to unzip it; I wanted to see his face. But I knew from my brother-in-law's tensed jaw, my mother-in-law's uncharacteristically dazed expression, and of course, the professionals in front of me that I could not ask this. I watched the gurney pass and suppressed a yearning to rest my hand on the sterile shroud. He would be cremated, so, that was that.

The bathroom opened onto the bedroom. I hesitated and opened the door. At that instant, I was reminded that it is possible to have several simultaneous and contradictory thoughts, a true mixture of feelings. For in front of me was something that, had I heard about it in advance, would likely have inspired a very different reaction than I experienced.

Before me lay what can only be described as a pool of blood, spreading to the corners of the small room and beginning to congeal at the rim of the shower stall. Thick, glossy, a profound red like no other. Strewn about, soaked with this blood, was Tom's typical weekend attire: worn, tattersall button-down, an old pair of khakis, black socks. In a corner were the objects he always, in the two decades I'd known him, carried in his breast pocket: a small date book and a sharp, yellow number-two pencil resting against a fallen pale blue towel.

The simultaneous thoughts came steadily. As if I were watching myself from a distance, I felt I ought to be shocked or torn with grief. He had apparently suffered—from what—a stroke? a fall? We had not heard the details yet.

And it occurred to me that I should also be disgusted. The scene in front of me immediately evoked Alfred Hitchcock or Stephen King: the pool of blood, a streak of a handprint along the white tile wall, a thick silence, unmistakable red splatters on the shower curtain. I thought, knowing how odd a thought it was, that this was exactly like those dramatic renderings. But I also knew that I could not escape that imagery. If we have been fortunate in life, movies and horror stories may be the only familiar, if melodramatic reference for an overwhelming event like this.

But those were passing thoughts devoid of emotion; I actually felt neither disgust nor shock. Something else overwhelmed me:

a feeling of grateful awe, a quiet regard for a space that felt sacred, and a peculiar, fleeting sense of immanence that may be what people describe as a religious experience.

This was the last of my father-in-law, I thought, the last of my friend of a quarter century. Part of him was still there in that room in the most intimate way—his blood from the very interior of his body, the red and the white cells, the platelets—maybe even a remnant of the leukemia that swept his life away in those past six months.

I suddenly had the most atavistic and unprecedented urge. I wanted to take up some of that blood and warm it in my hands, even to touch it against my face.

I must be crazy, I thought. But I knew I was not. People secretly bury their faces over months in the last blouse that a deceased loved one wore, avoid changing the sheets, inhale a familiar scent. But this is not only sensory and emotional; it is not an effort to retain a memory. There is something more.

I was as close to the last of this person's life—the edge of death—that one can experience: actual life's blood.

Is this what some ancient rituals, the reliquaries, St. Catherine's bliss, were about? Would everyone feel this immanence before the stark humanity of this pool of blood, this pencil that rolled along the floor and came to rest against a towel?

Judaism complicates my views of blood. Traditionally, the dead body, along with the substances it exudes, is *tameh*, usually translated as "impure." Preparation of the body for burial includes cleaning and sitting with it, making it *tahor*, or "pure." But Tom's body was gone.

If I could handle this fully tameh substance in a ritual way though, maybe it would be transformed. It would become tahor. I have heard that an encounter with this sacred gray area between life and not life, between the most *tameh* and the most *tahor*, can create holiness, kedushah.

These notions hovered among my thoughts.

I did not, of course, touch the blood. Not in the twenty-first century, secular climate of invisible hazards and mountains of waste. Although I knew I'd be unlikely to catch a disease, I deferred to the rules and my rational self, anticipating the arrival of the gloved and suited experts who would come clean it away, dispose of it properly.

So, I took a step back from the lintel and, as instructed, silently estimated the dimensions of the room and made mental notes of the extent of the waste and the damage.

When I finished, though, I could not tear myself away. Something caught my breath. There was something more in that room than awe and remembrance.

I am ordinarily a quite empirically minded person and, at most, an agnostic. Yet I stood there thinking that I might be witnessing Tom's soul. It lingered in those cells and seeped away while the blood hardened. Maybe this is why some believe that the soul rises. My friend was not completely gone; here, he was still tangible.

But skepticism battled sensation. And he didn't believe in souls, I'm pretty sure.

The cleaning service was late. When I was not needed downstairs, I climbed the stairs again, not telling anyone, not wanting them to think me morbid, self-indulgent, or disrespectful. But it was the opposite, and I wished I could pray. I wished that prayer meant something to me.

Later, in the kitchen, my mother-in-law talked to me about some details of the next few days. I fixed her a small plate of fruit and cheese.

We were quiet for a while; her sons were at the funeral home arranging things.

"What is shiva?" she asked out of the blue. I looked at her, surprised, this woman who took on Quaker ways when she married. I explained that it is the seven days that Jews sit at home after the funeral of a close family member. We neither work nor tend to usual tasks; people visit and bring food, and we recite the Mourner's Kaddish.

"That is interesting," she said.

"Would you like to do something like that?" I asked.

"No, I could never sit home."

"Perhaps we could bring you some meals, though, and eat with you if you like," I said.

"That would be good," she said, "Thank you." We sat in silence again. I scraped the dishes and placed them in the dishwasher.

Images of the quiet bathroom returned to me throughout the day and part of the next week before the funeral and, with those images, a visceral tenderness for life. I grasped for it, just beyond the periphery of my awareness, at the edges of the quotidian. For it was an elusive sensation; work and conversation dissipated it. In the mundane, it was lost. I felt it most strongly standing at the threshold of that room. It was neither disgust nor horror nor grief, but a peaceful sense of awe and love and something beyond words. Later, it was imbued with sorrow.

As we whisk away the dying and the dead in modern life, such profound moments are rare. Day to day, we may forget that we yearn for these moments, just as we yearn for rituals that contain our sorrow and our beauty.

26

Visiting the Graves

I RECOGNIZE THAT MY LACK OF NORMAL HOLIDAYS in 2020 was not the worst tragedy in all the world's tragedies that year, but I felt adrift as I anticipated the autumn holidays. I couldn't have my usual crowd over for festive meals or be with my community or family. Maybe I'd make a brisket just for myself, call my family, and light some candles. Indulge in self-pity.

Or maybe I wouldn't bother doing anything.

As the holidays approached, though, my melancholy gave way to a kind of anxiety—a more motivating emotion, I find.

I needed to do something to distinguish the sacred time. I wanted to feel like I was in the stream of history, religion, and tradition. And it needed to be tangible, sensory. Ritual is like that—the scent of spices or incense, the taste of sweet wine, the sound of rising song and the rhythm of a chant, the feel of one's body immersed in clean water—all add to the feeling that something meaningful has happened.

It is customary to visit the grave sites of close relatives the day before the High Holidays. I had never done that, so I tried to scheme a way to visit my father's grave in Connecticut. But travel seemed forbidding at that time, and what would I do if I could go? Stand there for ten minutes, say a prayer, and turn around and drive the four and a half hours back home?

A childhood friend's father had died a year prior and was buried in the same cemetery as my dad. My friend had told me she'd "visited" my father when she went to her father's grave that August. I was grateful. She knew that at the end of her father's funeral ceremony the previous year, I'd tried to find my father's grave marker. It should have been in the neighborhood of his old friend (her father), but I couldn't find it. The rabbi even stayed to help me, and he couldn't find it either. I gave up and went to visit with my friend and her family.

That autumn, it felt increasingly important to visit the graves, but whose? Where?

Then it came to me, a modification of the traditional ritual that might fulfill my desire for some semblance of spiritual connection during the High Holidays, some transcendence away from the screens and isolation.

Across the street from my mother's assisted living residence, not that far from me, is a historic graveyard. (Yes, the dark humor had not been lost on my siblings and me when she moved to this place: a facility not only with fastidious care but also a graduated system of assistance on site, from independent living through nine levels of support, then full assistance, then hospice, then—right across the street—burial. All within a stone's throw! Of course, she'd eventually be buried next to my father, in Connecticut. But we relied on such sardonic humor.)

I'd taken walks in this cemetery, in addition to the few funerals I'd attended there. The serene, wooded landscape felt a world apart from the nearby shopping center, office complex, and interstate highway. It's a historic preservation site from the early nineteenth century and an arboretum as well, with shaded paths through oak allées and up gentle slopes flanked by clusters of shrubs and flowering plants. There are more than three thousand botanical species listed, and the place is known for the historic personages buried there. I liked strolling through the special grave sites, names and dates in various languages and scripts etched on stone, a Veterans' area, a "green" burial site, and even a pet interment area.

This cemetery would be a felicitous place to visit before the holidays. Even in normal times, few people took walks during the week, and during the pandemic, there were no tours of historic graves, no bird-watching, and few people would be driving through or leaving flowers. The cemetery would be peaceful.

I've always liked graveyards: the scattered, tilted eighteenth-century family stones next to an old farmhouse in rural New Hampshire, the lone gravestone that I stumbled upon in the woods in Georgia, the grand obelisks in the nineteenth-century cemeteries, the flat stones in Quaker fields next to my children's Friends' schools, the familiar names in a fenced-in site in downtown Philly: people like Deborah and Benjamin Franklin.

I especially liked strolling the small graveyard on Cape Cod, where we went in the summer, with its classic tympanums and caps, all sinking into the earth. I liked the faded dates; the stylized willows, angels, and winged skulls, softened by the Cape's salty wind; names echoing the heyday of New England fishing communities: Jedediah, Increase, Abigail, Constance, Charity, Chastity (and the Other Virtues). Also, a row of graves with the same dates of death, all young men and boys, which signaled a storm that capsized their boats and drowned them. Scattered through the yard are also diminutive stones with faded lambs and swallows above a birth and death date both within a week or a day: the infant death, so common then. And the late twentieth-century graves, with facing benches and ages and dates, perhaps signaling one of the plagues in our time: all young men, all from the 1980s and 1990s, likely victims of AIDS.

In the corner of this Cape Cod graveyard sit a few simple markers. Little stones rest on their tops. The first time I saw these pebbles at a distance, I was surprised, but the inscriptions and stars of David confirmed my guess: these were the graves of Jews. The custom is to leave a stone to show you've been there. I'd forgotten that Jewish people had settled on the Cape.

It was comforting to see that others had left this little remembrance, a tiny gesture of connection with an unknown person. Long ago, such stones may have been intended to keep souls in and evil beings out of the grave. I prefer the simple, enduring interpretation: we have marked our visit. I like seeing that others have been there, and I often leave a stone, even on a stranger's grave.

So, the day before Rosh Hashanah, I would take a walk in the historic cemetery after visiting my mother. My former in-laws were buried there, and I hadn't recalled visiting their graves since their deaths, thirteen and six years prior. And though they were not Jewish, they were relatives.

Gliding at the requisite fifteen miles per hour through the gated entrance on that warm September morning, I was aware that I was both accustomed to and still surprised to see signs reminding us to stay six feet apart. There seemed to be some graveyard humor in there. I wondered what workers at the cemetery thought when placing the sign requiring us to wear masks when visiting the dead.

Outside the main office, a single car was parked, and an antique, horse-drawn hearse sat decoratively on the lawn. I decided against asking for directions to the graves and, instead, looked on my phone for the cemetery website and a map.

I first searched the site for records of where my former in-laws were buried. This took the better part of a while without success, so I called my former husband, their son. "Next to a conservatory or something, as I recall," he said. Conservatory. That should be obvious. I'd just follow the signs to the conservatory, park my car, and walk in a systematic circle around the conservatory until I found my in-laws.

Signs led me and my car along curving roads with names like West, River, and Memorial Drive, Bridge Road, none of which were eponymous. Black-and-white signs sported arrows that pointed to sections of the cemetery: Belmont, Ashland, Woodlawn, and the elusive Conservatory, but the sectors themselves were not labeled along the way. It was hard to tell which way to go at intersections since some road signs had the "Wizard of Oz" scarecrow's conundrum with arrows pointing in both directions, and some turns had no road signs at all. I found myself making U-turns in cul-de-sacs, backing out of one-way paths, maddeningly close, it seemed, to the conservatory, but then on the same circular drive, passing the same ambiguous arrows.

In the apocryphal words of the Down Easter, "You can't get there from here," appropriate, as my in-laws loved the coast of Maine.

I needed a more specific location.

Despite the 1869 founding of this cemetery, maybe they'd entered the twenty-first century and had a search app. Bingo. I stumbled on a records option and located my mother-in-law's grave site: Summit 67. My real mission could commence.

I just needed a good map. I found one online with letters and numbers marking each sector, building, and landmark, but without a key indicating what this alphanumeric system referred to. And no road labels. I squinted at the thing. That oblong building might be a conservatory.

I took a deep dive into internet archaeology. Yet another map: a charming diagram in early internet blue-and-white that resembled a schematic of an amoeba colony. It had new information— sector names—but no street or building names.

A third map had street names. Good. But no sectors. I tried toggling between the sector and the street map, but I'm not good at spatial things and my short-term memory seemed to have been obliterated by the circles I'd been driving in.

Maybe I could find a map that had both street names and sectors on it.

Ah. Here we go. One with microscopic labels of streets, landmarks, sectors, and buildings. I squinted and discerned that there was a bell tower next to the conservatory, and Summit sector was next to that. How hard could it be to find a bell tower?

Finally. I faced a bell tower with a conservatory next to it. Now, I'd just drive down the road that appeared to abut Summit sector and park right there. I commenced. The bell tower should be on my right, the road next to the sector on my left, but since I can't turn objects over in my mind, I turned the map upside down so that the bell tower, road, and sector in the map matched my physical orientation. I started driving to where my dear relatives should be buried, but seconds away, instead of pulling up to a peaceful row of relatives-by-marriage, I was on a grand driving tour of mausoleums.

Greek revival, International, Baroque, even Egyptian style. I amazed myself: I remembered my architectural history from my college years. I also admired angels and cherubs atop plinths and stopped to read the arboretum's tree labels: Japanese white pine, European beech, American holly, sugar maple, flowering pear. It was lovely. I was getting impatient.

This wasn't the first time I'd been thwarted in looking for a grave. Why were cemeteries always mazelike, inscrutable? Moreover, why did I always get lost? I recall more than one funeral when I drove around in circles, trying to figure out where Maple Grove or Section Six was, arriving at the last minute to the graveside. The maps always looked like they'd been drawn by hand and mimeographed in the 1960s. I'd arrive in my dark dress, breathless and a bit sweaty, wanting to focus on the somber occasion but feeling like I did when I was late to the opera and everyone else was seated, programs rustling, the scent of Chanel and Campari wafting judgmentally from a well-coiffed woman next to me.

I circled back to the bell tower. According to the map, this mausoleum should be to my back (it was); the bell should be in front to my left (it was); the conservatory, in front to my right (it was); and below that, the grave site (unclear). But the street name was all wrong.

I was ready to give up, but I was on a mission. Not for the dead—I don't believe my visit really mattered to them. The mission was for me and perhaps for the living extended family.

My search skills are rudimentary, I admit, but shouldn't this be easier, especially for people older than I?

Being the twentieth-century girl I am, it hadn't occurred to me until this point that there might be an electronic "button" for directions that maybe linked to a "real" driving map. Somehow, I found actual GPS directions to the actual grave, with the familiar map and its reassuring pulsing dots leading to my destination, indicated by a red pin. Another bingo. I peered at the image, drove slowly, but the charming, road names in the cemetery weren't on the map.

Maybe walking would be easier; the driving paths, which seemed to lead me and my poor orienteering skills astray, would be irrelevant. I was so close. I pulled the car into the parking lot next to the bell tower and got out.

I oriented the phone like a divining rod, pointed toward the red pin and me, the large pulsing dot, a few blue dots away. I felt foolish doing this, as I do when using a phone to go two blocks in a strange city when I suspect I've gotten turned around, instead of ambling, using the sun to orient east and west, or getting wonderfully lost, finding something new, asking directions. But this was not some existential, meandering journey on a new continent. Or maybe it was. Maybe this whole having-trouble-finding-the-site was part of my pre-New Year's ritual.

The directions indicated two minutes on foot to destination. I started walking on a road and followed the electronic, blinking blue breadcrumbs. And of course, I had to turn ninety degrees to the correct direction.

Finally, onto the soft grass, toward a low row of stones. I put my phone away and started to see familiar surnames of my in-law's family: old Philadelphia Quaker names.

And there they were, side by side, two modest markers. I teared up unexpectedly, seeing their full names next to each other: unadorned graves with just the names and dates of birth and death. I knelt and placed the palm of my hand gently on the cool gray stone. It was quiet. I listened to a distant cheep of a cardinal, the murmur of cars on the road beyond the gates. I pulled two small objects from my jacket pocket.

I wondered for a moment if it was permitted, but placed the seashells, one each, on the top edge of the small gravestones.

The shells were lighter than stones; a swift breeze or rain could knock them off. But no matter. It was all ephemeral. I would leave a fitting tribute.

The shells were from a glass jar in my home office. One, a pale pink spiral, the partial interior of a sea snail's shell, was from the Caribbean where my in-laws had loved to snorkel. Over a simple lunch, they delighted in adding to their life lists of fish they'd seen, consulting their well-worn guide, sharing their remembered bounty with us. I wasn't much of a snorkeler, preferring to take long walks on the beach or swim in a quiet cove. I used to bring home just one or two tiny or broken shells each year; I didn't want to denude the beach or take anything away from the protected park.

The other shell, also a sea snail's, also broken, was thin, delicate. The interior was streaked glossy brown and cream, like shiny glaze on good china. I believe this one was from a beach in the French town where my family lived when my children were little, where my mother-in-law had visited.

Better to use the shells for this ritual than to let them gather dust in my office. Anyway, this was more meaningful than keeping a mishmash collection.

And it seemed fitting to use a shell rather than a stone. The shells not only marked my visit but memorialized my in-laws' passions and identities. They both loved nature, things from the sea, and objects others might discard as seemingly worthless. And they would have appreciated the lack of perfection, the broken beauty.

I stood there awhile, enjoying the shells balanced on the narrow graves in the quiet grove. The soft color of the shells stood out against the dark-gray stone and emerald grass. Looking at the small spiral shapes suddenly reminded of the customary New Year's challah, also round and spiraled, symbolizing the circle of the year, of time, and some say, a crown—the royal crown of the seasons—the Days of Awe, the High Holidays.

Usually, I am against taking pictures or videos during rituals, even weddings. But I've often been outvoted on those rules, and though part of me thought it unseemly, I wanted this to be a communal, shared experience, even at a distance. I took a picture, sent it to the family, said a silent sort-of prayer, and walked away.

I strolled through the cemetery. It was cool beneath the trees despite the summery September day. Inspired by my ritual, I searched—in vain—for the small Jewish part of the cemetery, hoping to place a stone on a stranger's grave. But I'd apparently used up my orienteering luck for the day. Besides, this was not a task to accomplish; there was no reason to do more.

At a pedestrian entrance to the cemetery, monarchs and black swallowtails lingered on the swaying, pink milkweed and orange butterfly weed. I felt refreshed, less sorrowful and anxious about not having a proper New Year's that year. The brisket, the silver candlesticks, the lively table, the quavering voice of the woman behind me at in-person services would come around again in another year. That year, placing a shell on a gravestone was enough.

27

Writing to the Dead

AFTER MY FATHER DIED, I was surprised to find myself occasionally talking to him. My whispered, one-way conversations and chats in my head were a little embarrassing, but a book that I thought he would've liked, an accomplishment at work that was related to his interests, my children's progress in life, or just an emotional state sparked my spontaneous words.

These solo conversations, rare as they were, soothed and intrigued me. I asked for his advice, thanked him, pleaded for help and comfort, told him I wished he was around. I don't believe in an afterlife or that he heard me, but this continued for years after his death.

I certainly didn't expect an answer, yet these chats—sometimes a simple plea—filled me with profound appreciation, joy, a good kind of sadness, and a sense of what is important. After a while, I stopped thinking that my behavior was strange. Rational people do talk to dead relatives or friends; it's part of the normal grieving process and, for some, continues past the first mourning period. Our dear ones continue to have a psychological presence; perhaps this is what people mean when they say the beloved dead become part of us.

Chatting with my dead father was fine, but at some point, I started writing to him, too. I'd write to him because I was distressed, elated, confused, or just because I knew Dad would have understood. The letters ranged from a few sentences to multiple pages, sometimes rendered slowly over days, months, or years. The tangibility of a letter offered more than a talk, and while I engaged in this practice rarely, it became a meaningful act.

Of course, the letters never got posted, but writing a letter to someone who will never see it is freeing. You don't need to concern yourself with commas and all that; you can state things bluntly, say things you'd never otherwise say, let whatever rises to the surface find a place on the page. It can be cathartic. In that sense, writing to the dead resembles journal writing and other solo scribbling. And sometimes, my letters to Dad were just that: an unedited outpouring. But usually, I chose my words carefully, though I didn't edit per se. The rush of a journal entry may unburden us, but there is something about a letter, which requires you to communicate to another person, that can transform scattered or bottomless emotions and inchoate thoughts. And it is directed outside the self; the letter to the dead is, strangely, social.

While he would never read these, I imagined my father doing so; therefore, I had to at least pretend to communicate, though it didn't feel like pretense, and I was not talking to myself. Not only because it's my habit as a writer but also because picking the precise words *as if* addressing a live someone clarified my thoughts, added to my happiness and soothed my pain. Imagining my father as I wrote to him deepened my gratitude for what he gave me and my family.

These letters were a reverence for my dad's life and a reminder of my own blessings, and they helped me through darker moments or missing him. Further, the intimacy of the letter—private thoughts put on paper with the intention of someone holding and reading them, even in imagination—made me feel closer to him, whatever that means for someone who doesn't believe in spirits.

It also helped sustain my memories as I imagined him reading and reacting to the letter. His life, his self, continued to enrich my life, and the letters added to that.

While it sometimes shifted my mood, writing to the dead was less therapy and more ritual, and different from regular letters that might repair a relationship or communicate ideas. Writing to my father emerged as a ritual to honor him and deepen memories, to give meaning to the loss and to my day-to-day life without my father. At times, as I wrote the letters, I sensed a meaning beyond words. It was an everyday act rendered sacred through its transcendent purpose.

Writing had always been a way for me to sort out feelings, figure out a difficult conversation, or record experiences, so writing to my dead father came naturally. Especially earlier in life, I used writing as an emotional outlet. But there was also a tradition of letter writing in my family. During the Korean War in the early 1950s, my father was a medical officer stationed in Korea. He and my mother had just gotten married, and for the nine months they were apart, they wrote every day, sometimes twice a day, in the end, totaling a million words. Decades later, my mother edited these into a book.

Especially when we were young, my siblings and I exchanged letters with grandparents, cousins, parents, friends. Apparently, my maternal grandfather had required my mother and my uncle to write letters home from their summer camp in the Poconos in the 1930s and 1940s. My parents didn't make me write home, but as a child at overnight camp in Maine, I loved using my stationery embossed with flowers, turtles, or smiley faces, and I crammed as much information and earnest observations about life as could fit on the page. I often added a special sticker to the envelope's seal. I also corresponded regularly with my first cousin in Baltimore (and later, between our colleges), sent poems to my grandmothers, and wrote lengthy letters to a camp friend during our teens and twenties. She and I filled dozens of pages with our plans, heartbreaks, philosophical musings, book reviews, and complaints. In young adulthood and later, my siblings and I sent letters on airmail stationery and aerograms (which went extinct in the late 1990s) home to our parents, postmarked from Dakar, Haifa, San Francisco, Rome, Quito, Sydney, Kyoto, Aukland, Boston. Later, on sabbatical in southern France, I composed daily emails as if they were "real" letters, detailing cheeses and seasonal markets, our avuncular landlord, the challenges of getting my younger one into preschool, and the charms of our tiny, stuccoed rental, surrounded by wild rosemary and vineyards.

My letters to the living were sometimes meaningful, but as a ritual act, writing to the dead resembled prayers that address a god as "you." In many religions, there's no actual "you" in the sense of a god in front of us, but we address the divine entity anyway. Perhaps notions of gods are so elusive that we need to personify them in our prayers, even if, like me, we do not believe in a personified god or any god. We are social creatures; maybe it's natural to address a plea or an appreciation as if to a person. Although many prayers address "God," the words for "prayer" in some languages—for example, Hebrew—are reflexive verbs, implying prayer is something we do "to" or "with" ourselves. I just sit with the ambiguity: I don't need to decide or figure out to "whom" I'm praying; the prayer matters in itself and creates meaning or yields gratitude, wonder, rejuvenation, yearning, and a clearer sense of sorrow. I say the prayer *as though* I'm addressing someone, just as I addressed my deceased father in letters, as if he were there.

I do not want to suggest that my letters to Dad were necessarily prayers—nor that he was a god! Rather, this analogy illuminates part of why I came to see writing to the dead as a ritual. The process matters.

What follows are sections from letters I wrote to my dead father over a few years.

Dear Dad,

I missed you today while I was reading Ruth Bader Ginsberg's collection, In My Own Words. *She includes an excerpt from a buffo opera she and Justice Scalia wrote, and I suddenly was overcome with sadness, thinking how the confluence of opera, law, and humor would have appealed to you and how I wished I could share it with you. But I smile as I write this, for I can also imagine you saying how different and appealing things were then in the Court—two justices, often writing diametrically opposed opinions but enjoying this bit of creative, funny, and erudite frivolity. They were friends. You believed in communicating across the aisle and listening with curiosity to those we disagree with.*

[weeks later] And how I would love to tell you about my forays into medical humanities and how I learned all of this from you first by your example. You were a surgeon, musician, sculptor, lawyer, etc., etc., etc., who loved poetry. I realized after the fact that I am bringing it all together, defying the artificial distinctions among disciplines and the cult of expertise.

[7/6/18 et alia] Watching Wimbledon while I was on the stationary bike at the gym (both activities being extremely rare for me), I remembered your exclamations to the players on TV: look at that serve, beautiful, wow, can you believe it!

But it has been difficult for me these days, Dad, to "just be kind," as you so often reminded us, particularly later in your life when you said it frequently. Someone has hurt me badly, so I hope you would understand that pain can express in bitterness or meanness. I'm trying though.

[. . .] Damn! I just "discovered" the poet Donald Hall, and then he died this week. Not sure if you ever read his work, but it is passionate, of the "do not go gently" variety, and exquisite in its attention to detail, as Billy Collins does. You would like it.

It's exactly one month before my 60th birthday and feels portentous, a little sad. Hall was 89, the same age as you when you died, and yes, he was from New England, where you and Mom raised us. Like you, he adored his wife and writes not only of her illness but of her work (she was also a poet), her cooking, and his erotic feelings for her. I think you shared that all with Mom, too. I have to admit, reading all of it, I wish I had that kind of relationship with someone—like yours with Mom; like Hall's with his wife.

But isn't this one of the reasons we read poetry? To feel, to gain insight, to travel in the liminal space of words and understanding and feeling and of our souls?

I'm talking about artists dying, so here we go: last year, Derek Walcott, another favorite of yours (and mine) died. A summer wind in Philadelphia, muggy as the Carib, soft as a velvet collar, ruffles the pages on my desk.

In the past few years, some of my authorial touchstones— a Canadian novelist, an actor, a playwright and multiple poets—left this earth. You appreciated many of them, too, Dad, and many were your generation. It's that time of the century, I guess. This week, Paul Taylor; last week, John McCain; and on and on. I read about them, look at pictures, and feel the cord that holds me to my own past fray. You and Mom, perhaps you especially, Dad, brought the work of many of these artists and writers and luminaries into our lives. And when they die, I feel another small light go out in the yard, a flash of the firefly, reminding me of our frail humanity.

These things are important.

For example, Paul Taylor was my first favorite dance company and had in his repertoire the first choreography that brought me to tears. "Esplanade"—I watched the skimming dancers, heedless, run full speed downstage to be caught in a swan dive by another, just at the edge of the orchestra pit, and the music (Vivaldi?) seemed to compel the dancers one after another as they entered and exited, passing each other at full speed, mere inches apart, leaping head and arms first into another's waiting arms. I was breathless watching, there is a pure

*joy and beauty to this piece, and I have seen it many times. You
also loved this kind of dance.*

*When they are all gone, what will I feel? There are, of course,
younger ones waiting in the wings. But once your generation is
gone, perhaps I will look at my contemporaries and watch us
fall, each in our own time.*

*I also wanted to tell you that my dearest childhood friends'
fathers died recently—Bob, Walter, Ken (though I never called
them by their first names in those days!)—all in less than a
year, all in their 90s. Their names were so typical of that generation. You were friends and neighbors with them. Ken's daughter posted the memorial service online, with a slide show and
remembrances. A life well-lived, in a way we might now think
of as conventional, but truly a good life, a good man. You and
he shared many values and a strong sense of humor and fierce
love of family, despite one of you being a Midwestern Lutheran
and a Republican (of the old sort, before the Trump era), and
the other an East Coast Jew and a Democrat. Something's gone
with that, too, don't you think?*

*You would've appreciated Ken's memorial, which included
trumpet music, his favorite instrument, I believe. And I know
you would've smiled if you could've heard what your middle
daughter, Laurie, did at your one-year yahrzeit memorial:
blasted an opera recording across the cemetery. You would've
loved it.*

Thanks for listening, Dad. More later.

Love,

Wendy

Writing to my dead father came easily. If I felt sad writing, it
was a clean kind of sadness, the kind that makes you appreciate
life. Writing to him was edifying, even when it arose from diffi-
culty, and I relished those rare occasions. Perhaps it's because he
died in old age, with love and without pain. Perhaps it's because

our relationship had mellowed over the years, and by the time he died, it was unfettered from old complications.

Not so, my letter to G.

It was several decades after G.'s death when I decided to write to him, and it was not easy. In fact, I avoided it for months once I considered doing so, and it hadn't occurred to me to write to him until I'd written some letters to my father. In truth, it hadn't occurred to me until I started working on this essay, but once the thought came, I realized why I must, and soon, why I was avoiding it.

I'd actually written to G. a lot when we were young. In fact, as young boyfriend and girlfriend (very young!), we scrawled pages and pages to each other after he left for college. For some reason, I had forgotten about those letters until I thought about writing to him, the deceased "him." How could I forget? The letters had filled an entire banker's box, though I had discarded them—except one—at some point.

But this would be no love letter, no frenzied flight of imagination and passion-filled poetry. The time for earnest love letters with purple prose overflowing the page was long past, as was an epistolary dissection of our relationship, gone these many years.

While the urge to write to him arose spontaneously and continued, that urge was accompanied by dread. So, why do it, I kept asking myself. Why bother? Why was it so hard?

We had not been a couple in more than forty years; we weren't even friends, particularly, after we broke up. It was all a youthful memory. Our floundering, naïve love had ended in a mess, and the relationship was, despite its passion and occasional felicity, a mess, too. But that was long ago, and we didn't see each other much, for years; after a certain point, I didn't even think of him much, except in passing. None of that really mattered anymore. Also, twenty-five years had elapsed since his death.

But these facts did not explain why I needed to write the letter or why it was so hard.

As I wrestled with this ambivalence, I realized that I had never truly mourned his death. On some level, I had known that but not attended to it. I had been shocked when I'd heard he had died. I had cursed the universe when I heard he had taken his own life. But I hadn't attended his funeral because I hadn't even known about his passing until sometime after. Although I was anguished for a while, I'd never grieved; I'd never spent time among his community of mourners. I had never reconciled the manner of his death. I had shrunk from the images of what his death might have been like and turned away from the thoughts of what he'd never do, never see.

But I needed to contend with his death eventually. The dead don't haunt us, but our unresolved grief might. Some resolution, some ritual, was necessary.

As I realized that I'd missed the chance to mourn and memorialize G. and that I had not reached some equanimity about the manner of his death, writing a letter became compelling. It seemed one of the few recourses, but I wanted it to be ritual, not therapy. Even if the letter turned out to be emotionally palliative, I wanted something more, something that honored him—and our youthful relationship—and that allowed me some sense of mourning, of peace.

Despite the considerable deliberation that I gave to starting the letter, I did not want its composition to be deliberate; rather, I wanted to write with abandon, with the full intention of writing to him in particular, simply as a man whom I'd known since he had been a boy.

The letter would mark his passing. I remember. You are remembered. You mattered. What follows is the letter.

Dear G.,

Where to start? Maybe, in our old, school auditorium where you gave me an enormous cardboard heart covered in red construction paper in front of the entire assembly. Embarrassing, but also, I discovered later that you had tucked pine needles into an envelope and taped it to the back of the valentine. You had saved some pine needles from the grove where we first kissed.

Where to start? Maybe, in the tiny office that summer before you left for college when we put together a summer newspaper for high school kids—and spent a lot of time making out, too.

Where to start these decades later, decades after the shock of your death, a chilling tidal wave that flattened me, that comes back to haunt me still? I see you frozen in time, the last time I saw you, when we were around 30. But I mostly think about you in high school, that wild boy with the wild long hair, faded green painter's pants, a skinny guy, loping along, looking at me out of the corner of his eye.

Why write now? Because at my sixth decade, I haven't properly grieved you. Suicide makes it hard to grieve.

Moreover, it's time to thank you. Not to be avoiding anymore the memory of the pain and the anger and guilt about your death, which I think you would understand but might wave away. But that's what people do: look for a reason for this kind of death, when, of course, there never is one; guilt reflects that fruitless search.

Where to start? Maybe by thanking you for saying that you thought my writing, my words at 17, at 19, were spectacular—you said this, you—who wrote and edited spectacularly. When I doubted my writing, I knew you were telling me what you truly thought. You had trouble masking the truth.

To thank you, too, for the passion. Yes, fumbling, yes, frustrating, but, yes, my dear. We were so young, and it was exuberant, "inappropriate" at times. But real.

To thank you also (though I know this is a complicated one), for being so wildly, crazily at the edge and doing and saying things others didn't, for taking me along for the ride sometimes, even when I was embarrassed or probably should have tried to stop you. Later, I realized that some of this was probably the incipient mental illness that ultimately, cruelly, killed you, but it was also real and true and, at times, fun and transporting. But I wish I'd known then that there are different kinds of wildness. I imagine your wry smile: no regrets, you say.

To thank you, also, also, for the poetry and the letters—those letters that we wrote every fucking day when you were away. On paper, handwritten, a stamp and an envelope, with your sometimes-good poems.

You were brilliant. In some ways, too brilliant, and you burnt out like a supernova. A gorgeous writer, photographer, and ultimately, a scholar, but the accomplishments are immaterial.

To thank you, too, for pulling aside the curtain on our small town, for showing me, even when I couldn't wait to leave, that it had been a magical place to grow up, that those 18 years should be cherished. I didn't appreciate that until later.

But where to start? Maybe in an icy lake in late January, when we really had no business swimming, but our bodies were so warm after.

But where to start? Maybe in my little apartment in grad school, where you tracked me down, on my birthday, to ask if the reason we'd broken up—years before, mind you—was because of our religious difference. No, that didn't matter, I said, it never had. You were so relieved when I said that. Your worry worried me—you'd never thought our religions were a problem, and neither had I. In that little apartment, I could see that you were struggling, holding onto sanity by your fingernails. That was the last time I saw you.

And that was the last time you brought me daisies for my birthday, as you always had.

But where to start? Maybe in forgiveness, especially for that time in my first year of college, when you humiliated me in the most brazen way. (Just as you'd expressed your love in that wild *and public way, back when we were teens.) I forgave you a very long time ago, but never had a chance to tell you. I forgive you it all, and I know that some of the hurt was because of things that were outside your control. I understand.*

Thank you, too, for dancing with me. You were a terrible dancer but uninhibited and exultant.

But where to start?

28

The Last Country

THE DAY MY FATHER DIED, I entered a foreign country. No sign marked a border. No road, no guidebook, no map.

In the early days, I wandered my childhood home—my mother's house—trying to get my bearings. I talked little, looked at old knickknacks and photo albums as if I'd never seen them before. At first, I couldn't even read, and writing was alien as the eulogy loomed. I considered a dedication I'd written to my dad for an old manuscript, but words that had seemed poignant at the time were unrecognizable.

I ordinarily love to entertain, yet arranging a fruit bowl seemed foreign. Visitors I'd known my whole life seemed to speak an unfamiliar language: pleasantries and words meant to console didn't sooth me. Instead, I felt like a wary toddler. Only food and sometimes sleep interested me, and I accepted affection from family.

The relatively few deaths I'd experienced—my grandparents, older family friends, even two peers—did not prepare me for the strangeness of this country. My father had been declining with Parkinson's disease, and I fully understood he would die soon, but no visible track marked the rocky ground. And I seemed to have forgotten to pack.

This felt like a threatening place as well. I managed the funeral and burial, with my eyes and ears fixed only on family, on the words, the casket, and the earth, but once I returned to the house, I had no desire to go out. It bordered on agoraphobia. So, I donned an odd kind of armor: the soft embrace of an old beige sweater, which I wore for an entire week, a minimum of hygiene and grooming, and pinned to my sweater, the torn, black mourning ribbon, my sole adornment.

In those first days of mourning, my siblings also seemed to revert to a kind of instinct. My brother cleaned out the basement down to the bone, sorting and discarding my father's accumulation of old suitcases, scrap wood, duplicate tools, and the detritus of fifty-three years in one house. My sisters cooked, fed and fussed over others. I seem to have gone to ground.

But watch a dog when you reach a dead-end path in the woods: see how she meanders, nosing for a hint of a trail. That was me, eventually.

My first guidepost appeared when the rabbi came to discuss the funeral and shivah, the Jewish ritual week of mourning at home that follows burial. He even provided guidebooks: a prayer book and a slim paperback, *Guide for the Bereaved*. I closely read the prescriptions and prohibitions, and like a naïve tourist who memorizes *bow rather than shake hands; turn left at the cathedral,* I read: *wash your hands before entering the house after the funeral; cover the mirrors* (we didn't, but I avoided looking in them when brushing my teeth or hair); *conversation should be muted.*

My old sweater apparently made sense, my desire to do "nothing," prescribed. I had permission to stay home and avoid entertainment, not to bathe or change clothes. During shivah, we were to be barefoot and sit on low stools, no better than other animals. Even my brother's inclination to clean out seemed primal and related to taharah, the ritual cleansing of the deceased's body.

The rituals sanctioned our yielding to mourning and its instincts. In fact, it turns out that the days between death and burial (called *aninut*) are intended to be a kind of suspended animation when family members can be fully in grief and do nothing but prepare for the burial, not even receive visitors.

I still roamed the house but with the guide and prayer book in hand like an inexperienced tourist clutching her dog-eared phrase book and crumpled map. Following the "rules," I started to look forward to the evening service when I felt a wave of prayer and song lifting me above the tides of grief. Amazed, I watched as my son calmly sang a Scottish air in memory of his grandfather.

In his memoir, *The Seven Storey Mountain*, Thomas Merton notes that his father's death occasioned an unbearable, animal-like suffering, but faith eventually rendered grief tolerable, even transcendent. Similarly, my rituals not only sanctioned mourning in the sense of giving permission but also *sanctified* it—imbued it with sacred meaning. The practices recognize our bewildered state, particularly in the first few days; they acknowledge the human condition in the face of death and make it possible to begin to pass through the dark country.

I began to do more than eat, sleep, and look at knickknacks. Like street signs in an increasingly familiar city, mourning's structure guided me, and a second track emerged through the fog: reading. The contemporary readings provided social and psychological advice, and I also read the prayers and psalms closely. Although I'd been generally familiar with the liturgy, I read it differently, finding in the words (or projecting onto them) how to be less of a stranger to grief. Even the phrases that used to seem hackneyed suddenly appeared clearer—all seemed to contain the geography of a broken heart.

Valley of shadow, mountains melting like wax, singing trees, roaring seas, jumping islands, and skipping hills, deserts in turmoil. We are exhorted to *rise from the dust and leave the valley of tears.* Of course, the ancient poets and mystics intended these as metaphors for "God's power," "the Israelites," or "the soul." But these images felt visceral, and I said every word and yearned for them to reach me. The prayers joined the rituals to become coordinates for orienting myself.

Though familiar in a way, a central part of the liturgy eluded me: Kaddish, which mourners traditionally recite for eleven months. At the graveside, I said the prayer aloud for the first time in my life, and though I fully recognized the words because I had heard them many times, the syllables felt alien, as did the knowledge that this was *me* saying it. All those years, I knew only in the abstract that I would someday be among those who stood when the rabbi said, "Those in mourning, please rise to recite Kaddish." As a child, I looked at mourners in synagogue with sympathy and furtive curiosity. Except for the brief refrains that congregants give, I had scrupulously avoided chanting the prayer—preserving it exclusively for a parent's death, as I had learned and had subsequently instructed my own children—to keep its incantatory power. But now I was thrust into the mourners' terrain, ushered along by the prayer's rhythm and syntax. Despite initial nervousness, I chanted it regularly, although whatever power it contained felt transient.

My stack of guidebooks grew. Like the liturgy, some poets comforted me, especially some of my father's favorites. I read and reread Stanley Kunitz's line, "I see the milestones dwindling . . . and every stone on the road precious to me." Mary Oliver's poems about the "soul" drew me in, even though I eschewed the idea of a soul. I wished I could tell Dad he'd left me clues to the shadowed country.

Despite my ritualistic and poetic guides, I was still lost. During the first weeks (and even later), the rituals sometimes struck me as pointless; the poetry, empty; my loneliness, overwhelming. And unlike an actual country, I was traveling through time, not space, and it was a bizarre kind of time: the first days progressed like the slow ticktock of a heavy grandfather clock, the prayers serving as the chime of the hours. And the following weeks seemed disjointed, slow.

Yet the rituals sanction a time structure: from the suspended animation of aninut to the seven days of shivah; through a thirty-day period (*shloshim*) that permits bathing, working, and additional activities; to an eleven-month period of modified mourning, after which one recites Kaddish on the anniversary of death and on some holy days. The expression "time heals" does not seem true to me, but as with jetlag or altitude, we adapt, and the ritual provides milestones, which the human psyche perhaps needs. There may be a spiritual impetus as well.

A. J. Heschel, the twentieth-century theologian and activist, said that in Judaism, time, not space, is sacred. We can pray anywhere and we worship no icons; the cycle of holy days, those of mourning, and most of all, the Sabbath, are sacred acknowledgements of time. God, he wrote, is "not in things of [material] space, but in moments of time," and "Time is the heart of existence."

Time became my ally, despite my continuing sense of standing still, and its religious markers shepherded me through the days and, hence, to months. Only my notes that I began at the end of the first week proved to me that shivah was really only a week, and shloshim, only a month, so slowed did this time feel. Like returning from a trip and reading my journal months later, I would not have otherwise believed the experiences were as I remembered.

Once I yielded to the primal behaviors and to the slow rhythms, I found rich texture in the days. With an odd kind of wonder, I noticed the detail on a small figurine, in the almond flavor of a pastry; even the smells seemed acutely, poignantly amazing. My eyes welled noticing my childhood backyard through a window: each swell and dip of the lawn, the tall oaks and great solitary boulders that we used to play on, the sound of a bird's insistent cry, and the knowledge that box turtles were beginning to stir from hibernation. Indoors, I noticed details of the house itself—the long wooden beams, cathedral ceilings, and the old mail "chute." Outside the kitchen windows, three infuriating squirrels hung from the bird feeder by their little claws, breakfasting. (You never did win your arms race with them, Dad.)

This sensibility reminded me of the first weeks of being abroad when you perceive novelty: the excitement in navigating narrow streets and mazelike markets, the smell of mounds of spices, the feel of fabrics and baubles. In my new, sad country, the sensations and full emotions were a gift of grieving.

During mourning, I recalled another line from Kunitz: "What makes the engine go? Desire, desire, desire." A handsome man paid a condolence call, and talking with him, I felt a flicker of something which I chose not to ignore. Even in the midst of flattening grief, the "engine" fires itself. This was familiar terrain.

Not only this spark of attraction but other inclinations also emerged. During services, my mind strayed to the aesthetic dimensions of the prayers. My father would have understood these distractions; though he respected tradition, he stood on neither ceremony nor false piety. And pleasure in music, poetry honored some of his passions.

The human animal needs novelty, society, sensuality. All these pull us along in this surreal country. Eventually, I was driven to write, to seek intellectual stimulation and company. Humor, art, and desire shimmered through the mist.

When I arrived back in Philadelphia, though, I seemed to regress, as if the drive across the borders of three states had brought me to another unknown language and custom. The world felt ominous outside the shell of my car, and I scurried to the safety of my house, glad there were a few more days of shivah when I would not have to go out. I reverted to the simple not doing, paging through old photographs and waiting for meals.

On Saturday, mourners are advised to say Kaddish at synagogue instead of home, to suspend mourning in favor of celebrating the Sabbath. I resented the six blocks to and from home but did it anyway, keeping my eyes to the ground, avoiding people I didn't know, watching my steps on the narrow sidewalk, thinking, literally, "Put one foot in front of the other." Part of me understood the wisdom of exiting the house and taking a break from mourning, but my neighborhood of twenty-five years provoked much more anxiety than I'd sometimes felt planning out a first bus route in a new, chaotic city.

When Shabbat ended, I was comforted by pinning the black ribbon to my sweater again. In the evening, people came bringing food for after the home service, and with friends and congregants sitting behind me in my living room, I heard their response to my call.

Over the following weeks, particular readings became more or less meaningful. I put Oliver to the side; her simplicity, which had comforted me at the beginning seemed insufficient to more nuanced emotion and my changing thoughts and memories, just as the basics of a new language become inadequate to describe abstract ideas: I was beyond *cup of tea, where is the train station,* and I favored more opaque, complicated poems.

The heightened sensibility remained. Driving home from taking my son to school in heavy traffic several weeks later, I felt none of the potential frustration; instead, the pink cherry blossoms and luxuriant magnolia buds appeared almost painfully beautiful, and even the yard signs popping up announcing spring open houses for schools imbued me with a kind of tenderness, as though I'd never seen the blossoms or signs before. Although I was not as productive as I wished in those first months, I relished these sensory details. Besides, it was all I could manage, like fumbling for the right coins or turning down the wrong, seemingly identical alleyways in a new city but also noticing the rich color and intense flavor of a just-picked pomegranate.

As with most long journeys, each week seemed to bring my body more in synchrony with the actual calendar and the real hours. My sense of vulnerability eased. Each Shabbat marked another week; the end of shloshim provided the first big milestone; and the occurrence of seasonal holy days punctuated the longer spans and magnified the changes I noticed in myself. Coming soon after my father's death, Purim, the Feast of Esther, was difficult, its levity painful. But a month later, though I, at first, dreaded driving back to my mother's house for Passover, the celebratory meal ended up being a poignant joy: I had been given Dad's former responsibility of leading the home observance, and we celebrated him as well.

My acculturation increased. After several months, I started to look forward to reciting Kaddish. I recalled how in the first weeks, I'd see other mourners in the congregation who seemed calm, even happy in their recitation, and I hadn't a clue how I could even stand up, never mind chant. And here I was relishing each word, noticing—quite late in the year—that it was an exultation not a dirge. I was no longer just repeating it as a mantra but also engaging with its meaning. Some weeks brought tears, but I stood.

Two, then three, and ten months passed, and I realized it was time to look up the Jewish calendar's date for the end of ritual mourning and for my father's yahrzeit, the anniversary of his death. I knew that when formal mourning ended, I would cross into another country without an itinerary or knowledge of the culture. What would it be like not to have the requirements of mourning? In the last month, I was a little sorry, nervous even, about the prospect of not reciting Kaddish regularly.

Of course, just when you think you understand a city's geography or a language, you get lost again. I realized I'd been taking for granted that everyone who shared the memory of my father would accompany me forward. But then, my father's best friend from childhood died, two months short of my father's yahrzeit. I realized anew that fewer and fewer people would remember my father. I would gradually become one of those few and would become a sign and signal for others. My own mortality flickered on the horizon in ways it never had. This is the last country, I thought.

It would never be finished, this accommodation. We wander off sometimes, not realizing we will need to find the trail again and again. But if we let ritual and time carry us, permit the animal instincts to take hold, it is perhaps clearer how to navigate the months of mourning.

My father didn't believe in an afterlife, and neither do I. But sometime during the year of mourning, an image came to mind: I imagined you, Dad, flying in your wheelchair to a cinematic heaven. Like Mary Poppins or Harry Potter, you dart among the clouds, and there are your parents, Rose and Hy, sitting in their light-blue, overstuffed living room chairs, ready to greet you. You three, the parents and the older man-child, are about the same age at that moment, since you died at around the same age. They embrace you, Rose with pride and her vice grip of a hug, Hy with his usual chuckling delight. And you are delighted to find everyone bobbing in their seats in this celestial terra incognita.

But the reunion is only a split second. You all scatter, your bodies and souls dispersed throughout the universe in tiny glitter, falling on us with sparks of grace and glimmers and whispers over the millennia and into *olam habah*, the world to come, and soon you settle in our peripheral vision, like the shooting stars in August above the Cape Cod home you loved, like the northern lights in a faraway country.

ACKNOWLEDGMENTS

Deepest appreciation to my literary doulas, readers and friends nonpareil, Emily Law and a dear, longtime friend who wishes to remain anonymous. Their editorial advice, unwavering support, grace, and humor made this book possible.

Thanks to Ana Hernandez and John Salt for providing details about their wedding, and Judy Kopman-Fried for the precious gift of her parents' story. Noah H. Shipley and Philip C. Bayer coached me on artwork, and Chrys H. Shipley righted some upside-down facts. For helping me find my mojo to launch this project, Marnie Rosenberg deserves credit.

Louise Bensen, Gail Heimann, Sonia Kane, Claire McCusker, Amy Stone, and Patty Wright: thanks, my dears, for the practical advice and pep talks. Grateful appreciation to Joan Marlow Golan for years of encouragement and writing advice and to Jennifer (Nifer) Hughes Brusca and Noah H. Shipley for reading select chapters. Suggestions from Anna Beresin, Eileen Flanagan, Judd Levingston, Abbie Salt, and Thomas F. Shipley smoothed the pre-publication process. Thanks also to Neal Beresin for his monthly poems, a blessing in bleak times.

Conversations with Bec Richman inspired some of my ideas about ritualized objects. Shai Gluskin reviewed some of my descriptions of Jewish practices, and Linda Holzman commented on an early draft of "Kedushah." I am grateful to Adam Zeff for concepts about prayer discussed in "Writing to the Dead," some of which appeared in his sermons in fall 2022.

Special thanks to my editor, Dan Crissman, who understood this project from the start. His patience and insight made this a better book. Anna Francis, Samantha Rose Heffner, Alyssa Nicole Lucas, Darja Malcolm-Clarke, and Pamela Rude at IUP fielded my many questions and shepherded the book through publication. I could not wish for a better team.

The following chapters were previously published as individual essays in a different form:

Horwitz, W., "White Coat, Black Book," *in-House*, July 2022, https://in-housestaff.org/white-coat-black-book-1976

Horwitz, W., "Kedushah," *Jewish Literary Journal*, August 2020 86: n.p. https://jewishliteraryjournal.com /creative-non-fiction/kedushah-wendy-horwitz/

Horwitz, W. A. "Narrow Bridge," originally published as "Elegy for the Tappan Zee," *Intrepid Times*, October 14, 2019, https:// intrepidtimes.com/2019/10/elegy-for-the-tappan-zee/

Wendy A. Horwitz's essays have been published in the *Philadelphia Inquirer, Afterimage, Neurology* (Humanities Section), *Jewish Literary Journal, Intrepid Times,* and *McClatchy-Tribune News Service,* among others. Originally trained as a pediatric psychologist, she teaches and lives in Philadelphia.

For Indiana University Press

Tony Brewer, Artist and Book Designer
Dan Crissman, Editorial Director and Acquisitions Editor
Anna Francis, Assistant Acquisitions Editor
Anna Garnai, Editorial Assistant
Samantha Heffner, Marketing and Publicity Manager
Brenna Hosman, Production Coordinator
Katie Huggins, Production Manager
Darja Malcolm-Clarke, Project Manager/Editor
Dan Pyle, Online Publishing Manager
Pamela Rude, Senior Artist and Book Designer
Stephen Williams, Assistant Director of Marketing